Ellice Hopkins

Work amongst working men

Ellice Hopkins

Work amongst working men

ISBN/EAN: 9783741191749

Manufactured in Europe, USA, Canada, Australia, Japa

Cover: Foto ©Andreas Hilbeck / pixelio.de

Manufactured and distributed by brebook publishing software (www.brebook.com)

Ellice Hopkins

Work amongst working men

WORK AMONGST WORKING MEN

PRESS NOTICES OF PREVIOUS EDITIONS.

"In her biography of James Hinton, Miss Hopkins proved that she possessed wide tolerance and high culture. The book before us shows that she has also an aptitude for that practical work among the poor in which less gifted women are often so successful. She has great sympathy with the poor, and understands, as those only can who have lived among them, their special trials and difficulties."—*Pall Mall Gazette.*

"Miss Hopkins' book is not exclusively concerned with her own work. It contains many valuable suggestions upon other matters connected with the class for which she has done so much; and we advise all who are interested in the poor to read it for themselves."—*Spectator.*

WORK AMONGST WORKING MEN

By ELLICE HOPKINS

AUTHOR OF 'LIFE AND LETTERS OF JAMES HINTON' 'WORK IN BRIGHTON,' ETC.

FIFTH EDITION

NEW YORK
THOMAS WHITTAKER, 2 & 3 BIBLE HOUSE
1884

CONTENTS.

		PAGE
I.	MY FIRST VENTURE	1
II.	MY FIRST CONVERTS	16
III.	INTELLECTUAL GOSPELS AND THE PEOPLE	31
IV.	MEN AND WOMEN	46
V.	EVANGELIZATION	63
VI.	SOCIAL DIFFICULTIES	97
VII.	THE SAVINGS QUESTION	138
VIII.	OVERCROWDING	169
IX.	CONCLUSION	174

CHAPTER I.

MY FIRST VENTURE.

'RELIGION is all very well for women;' from my earliest years I have detested that maxim of the great Emperor's. From a child I always counted the bare heads in church, and estimated the preacher's power according to their number. From a girl I had the strongest conviction that the Gospel of Christ was essentially for *men;* and that only so far as a man is in Christ and like Christ can he be really a man.

It was, therefore, with no small dissatisfaction and pain that I was constantly hearing from a number of respectable girls of my own age, whom I had gathered into a Bible-class at my own house, that their fathers and brothers, as a rule, went to no place of worship.

Skirting one of the Universities is a large and populous suburb where the mass of the working people live, and which from time immemorial had borne a most unenviable character. I fear it was a practical comment on the truth of that uncomfortable proverb, 'The nearer the church, the farther from God,' that so bad a district should adjoin one of the great head-quarters of the Church. I can myself remember the time when it was not considered safe, or proper, for a lady to penetrate its recesses alone. On one occasion my mother, having to make some business inquiries, asked a man who was standing in one of the main streets to direct her to a certain 'Gas Lane.' 'Yau'll find it on your right,' he replied; 'but it's a rum lot *you* are going among, old lady,' he added, with an uncomfortable stress on the pronoun, which is felt in circumstances of dubious peril to appeal forcibly to the imagination.

But having made up my mind to see if something could not be done to influence men as well as girls, it was this suburb, with its

MY FIRST VENTURE.

lawless population of roughs, that I chose as the sphere of my efforts. Youthful heroism, when combined with Christianity, even though it can no longer culminate in a St. Theresa, has still some few outlets left in these degenerate days, and is not quite reduced to the melancholy career our great novelist, George Eliot, accords it, as summed up in Miss Nightingale's words, 'of first marrying an elderly literary impostor, and then quick after him, an inferior sort of faun.'

Accordingly, one Tuesday evening at half-past five, I found myself seated in a cottage with sixteen men. Two or three of the district visitors, who had attended my Bible classes, had set to work with the enthusiasm with which only women can work, and, by dint of seasoning all their meals and part of their evening with my praises, had at last persuaded this limited number, with great difficulty, to come and hear me for themselves.

I suppose there is something essentially touching in a woman's speaking. I have rarely heard a woman speak but I have felt a strong unreasoning impulse to tears. 'I cried like a calf,' ('J'ai pleuré comme un veau,') said a leading Protestant in France, on hearing a lady friend of mine address some of the Paris chiffoniers in their own language; and the friend who went with me to my first meetings used laughingly to declare that she always took with her a large white pocket-handkerchief and spread it out on her knees, ready for instant action the moment I began. Perhaps it is that the woman's voice keeps so many tender home-tones, and has never been hoarsened at elections, nor in political meetings, nor in the streets, but is like an instrument on which only loving hands have played, and all our mother pleads with us in its gentleness. Certain it is, there were few dry eyes in that cottage on that Sunday evening.

I soon found out, however, that they did not like coming to a private cottage; so, as my clergyman was as anxious as I was for the success of the experiment, I decided to move at once into his schoolrooms.

The following Sunday, rather to my dismay,

I found the small room, which I had considered large enough to accommodate my audience, full to overflowing, and many men were obliged to stand and listen outside. After the address was over, I went up to one of my first hearers and expressed my regret that he had not been able to get into the room, adding that we would meet in a larger room next time, when I hoped he would be able to hear. 'Oh, thank you, Miss, I heard your 'scourse quite well through the door,' he exclaimed, enthusiastically. From which time we concluded that ''scourse' must be the feminine of discourse, a point of English grammar which Murray has failed to notice, owing, doubtless, to female speakers scarcely existing in his days, or, at least, being still subject to Dr. Johnson's opprobrious remark, 'Sir, a woman preaching is like a dog standing on its hind legs; the thing is not well done, but the wonder is it can be done at all.'

Seeing that the work was likely to outgrow my single-handed powers, I made my first effort to organize my meeting, and asked two or three

Sunday-school teachers to work with me. At first their work was chiefly to find out the worst characters and bring them to the meeting. One dapper little man, a Mr. B., was greatly delighted at my asking him to work with me, and promised he would do his best at my very next meeting.

The next Sunday, the friend who always went with me being ill, I started off alone, adding to, rather than lessening, my alarm by calling for a working-man on the way. This man I knew had resisted all efforts to get him inside a place of worship, or, alas! but too often, outside a public-house. But I had reached that convenient stage of terror which turns the corner and rounds upon courage, and felt perfectly reckless what became of me. Brought up, as I had been, in all the refined and intellectual life of an University, which, I sometimes think, more than any other separates one from the life of the people, I doubt whether at that time a sheeted spectre had the same unknown terrors for me as a rough in the 'too, too solid flesh.' And I knew that many were beginning to look grave, and question whether it was safe for a young lady to gather together a mass of lawless men, with the certainty that, if any outbreak took place, she would be powerless to control it. But, on the other hand, what was most evident to me was, that these men would come to me on the Sundays, and, as had been too well proved, would not go to any church or chapel. One other lady besides myself, a young clergyman's wife, had succeeded lately in getting together a certain number on a week-night,—her Sundays being fully engaged, —and was doing good work among them. But the worst men, the men who most want some humanizing influence, cannot be got to weekday meetings, they are too tired after their work to make the effort to come to what presents no attraction to them; while on the Sunday time hangs heavy on their hands, and to go to a meeting is a much less marked proceeding. Their uncared-for souls lay at my door, not at the doors of those who criticised me; my clergyman, to whom, if to any one, I owed obedience, urged the work upon me;

and, do what I would, I could not shut out the duty of welcoming them in the name of Our Lord. I had my earthly father's blessing, why should I doubt my heavenly Father's? If there is one truth I have grasped more strongly than another it is this: only be sure of your duty, and there must be an infinite store of force in God which you can lay hold of to do it with, as an engineer lays hold of a force in Nature and drives his engine right through the granite bases of an Alp. If you are sure that it is God's will you should do it, then 'I can't' must be a lie in the lips that repeat 'I believe in the Holy Ghost.'

> 'So nigh to grandeur is our dust,
> So nigh is God to man,
> When Duty whispers low, ' Thou must,'
> The soul replies, 'I can.'

As St. Theresa said, in answer to some objectors, when she set about founding a much needed orphanage with only three halfpence in her pocket, 'Theresa and three halfpence can do nothing; but God and three halfpence can do all things.' I was but the three halfpence, but

I might be used to redeem these men from the slavery of sin.

When at last I emerged from the dark street into the large well-lighted school-room, a scene presented itself which could only be witnessed in our own country, or that other great English-speaking land, America. The room was full of wild, rough men, some of them desperate characters enough, men who had never been known to come together in large numbers without some row taking place. I was the only woman in the room, entirely at their mercy, a mere inexperienced girl with the love of her Saviour at her heart, and wishful of saving others, but with nothing to oppose to their wild lawless strength but the invincible weakness of the divine. Yet nothing could be more orderly and devout than the simple service we held together, and when it was over, and they crowded around me to shake hands with me, and thank me, my own brothers could not have been more reverent and careful of me than these rough men.

As soon as he could get at me, my dapper

little Sunday-school teacher bustled up to me, and exclaimed, with a glow of self-satisfaction, 'I think I may say I was successful in my first endeavours in your cause, Miss. I brought you seven men,—all drunk,' he added, with a touch of gentle pride, in remembrance of my injunction to get the worst. And sure enough he had picked them out of a neighbouring public-house, and shored them up one after the other on a bench in a row, spending some hours and much patient ingenuity in this unprofitable task. Fortunately they did not tumble backwards, nor, like Cassio, take to talking fustian with their own shadow, nor in any other way disturb the meeting; enough of the man still being left in those seven beer barrels to make them feel thoroughly ashamed of themselves. But they always went by the name of 'little Mr. B's. first contribution.'

From the Sunday of my escape from the seven drunken men, my rough congregation increased a hundred or so at a time. At first I was for limiting the meeting to one large room, but my clergyman, delighted that the men of his parish could be got to hear the gospel, whether from man or woman, took the matter into his own hands, and flung open the folding-doors that separated the two large school-rooms, and both rapidly filled. As the fame of the meeting spread, men used to come streaming in from the villages round, some walking ten or twelve miles, till at last they stood packed as close as herrings in a barrel, from five to six hundred being crammed into a space meant for not much more than half that number. Most singular was the scene presented by the broad road leading to the Abbey school-rooms at half-past five, when the women-folk were mostly in-doors at tea; nothing but the heavy tramp! tramp! of men being heard, all converging to one spot.

After a few brief struggles I had overcome the great clothes difficulty. On the point of getting men to be content to go to heaven in their old jackets, my heart was much set. On one occasion I asked the mother of a grown-up son why he never came. She replied, 'He'd like to come, Miss, but he's no trousers.' 'But

I don't want his trousers; I want *him!*' I exclaimed, with an apparent fine indifference as to whether he came with or without those indispensable habiliments, which sorely tried my companion's gravity.

But soon, as the meeting was only for men, it became a sort of rough fashion to attend it. Mr. Darwin tells us that male birds have their bright plumage for the sole purpose of attracting the more dowdily-clad female. Certainly I found it so at my meeting. Their wives and sweethearts were not there to look at them, and the crowd was too great for me to see them, so they used to come in their working dress, and even sometimes in their shirt-sleeves. One old drunkard, however, used regularly to pay sixpence to get his clothes out of pawn on Saturday night, and regularly return them to durance vile as soon as the meeting was over.

But what a work it was! Truly, I had need of a strong faith in God, for my difficulties were great. In the first place, I knew that, young as I was, if once undergraduates were to take to coming to the meeting, it must come to an untimely end. On one occasion I espied one among the crowd, and, walking up to him, as courteously as I could I publicly turned him out; but another, seeing what I was after, deftly whipped off his gown while my back was turned, and sat upon it, and so completely baffled me. But my wishes having been thus strongly expressed, and the suburb being some little distance from the University, that peril soon came to an end; though to the last I was often amused by the wildest reports that had reached some distant friend,—how forty undergraduates had, on one occasion, come to mock, but remained to pray, etc., which, in a Dissenting organ, was magnified into a hope that I might 'prove the feeble instrument of bringing a knowledge of saving grace to a godless and unbelieving University.' The idea of that awful functionary, the Vice-Chancellor of the University, accompanied by his beadles and 'bull-dogs,' attending the Abbey school meeting, held by a young lady in that tabooed suburb, is one the wild profanity of which it requires a university-bred mind to appreciate.

But a far greater difficulty lay in the character of the men I had to deal with. With large numbers I was their only influence for good, the only voice that spoke to them of God and Christ. Out at their work all day, many of them never saw a clergyman or a district visitor. A good many came from sheer curiosity, and if I failed to make any impression on them I knew not whether the opportunity would ever come again, nor what desperate deed they might do. In the first year of my work a murder and a suicide took place not far from the door of my school-room. On one occasion six men came from a neighbouring village to 'hear the lady preach,' but as preaching was dry work in general, they provided themselves with a shilling a-piece, with the intention of turning into a public-house on their way back, and getting 'jolly drunk' in my honour. I am thankful to say that the word which met them was too strong for them, and they returned perfectly sober with the shilling safe in their pockets. Generally they took my adventurous plain-speaking very well. Once after I had had to speak very plainly of the sin and degradation of some of their lives, the want of true manliness among them, two men went away and walked side by side without saying a word till they reached their garden gates, when they turned and faced one another. 'Bill,' one was heard to say to the other, 'for the first time in my life I've been well licked, and that by a woman.'

'So have I—good night,' laconically rejoined the other, and bolted into his house.

But God only knows the unnecessary anguish I went through lest I had not been earnest enough; lest some unthought-of word of mine uttered more from the heart might have saved my brother; tormenting myself, like many another young soldier in the fight, instead of asking God for grace to do my best, and quietly leaving the issues and increase with Him.

CHAPTER II.

MY FIRST CONVERTS.

MEANTIME I was steadily going on with the organization of my meeting, and was slowly gathering round me a band of earnest helpers, both men and women. I was always reminding them that if I was the head they were the limbs, and that the head without the hands and feet would be helpless; so that they grew to feel that the meeting was theirs as well as mine; and we all worked with a will. Their part was not only to recruit for the meeting but also to watch for any who were impressed, and keep them back for the after meeting, and talk and pray with them, as well as to visit them in their own houses, or in some cases bring them up to me. Ultimately I was joined by Miss Macpherson, since well known in connection with emigration, and found her most helpful to my inexperience.

Very soon one of my right-hand helpers, a working-man, who had stood for seven years almost alone on the side of Christ in some large brick-fields, but now found himself a sort of spiritual father amongst his mates, who till then had led him a life of constant petty persecution, told me that seven working-men wished to lead a different life, and would like me to talk and pray with them. So they came up to my house, most of them, at the time I am writing, Christian men of more than ten years standing, but then in the glow of their first faith and their first love, with that simple, hearty, unreserved surrender of themselves to God common to working-men, but rare, at least in its outward manifestations, in more sophisticated ranks of society. I remember now one of those first prayers that welled out of a full heart, rude in language but deep and pure in feeling:—'O Lord, you know how I have been knocked about in the world, and grow'd up in publics, and never had any one to care for my soul, till our blessed hand-maiden came to teach us about our Saviour, and about our Father in heaven.'

Few, indeed, of us can realize the rough unhumanizing character of the lives of many of our working-men. Some, like this man, had lost their mother young. Many more, alas! might as well have been hatched by steam, as far as any mother's care and tenderness go, and would doubtless have echoed the young street Arab's sentiment, '*He* didn't see what good mothers were, 'cept to wallop a fellow.' And it is just this rough, motherless, uncared-for side of their lives which makes the influence of a refined and educated woman something to them which the most tender-hearted man can never supply. I would especially urge this fact on those who object to a woman working among men. Would that I could only think that these rough notes, written years after I have myself been laid aside from this work, might be the means of stirring up some lady, young or old, to try her influence over the working-men of her neighbourhood, and be to

MY FIRST CONVERTS.

some dusty, hard-toiling lives a gracious dew from heaven, 'twice blessed,' indeed; blessing her who gives and him who takes.

But my first prayer-meeting had its very funny as well as its solemn, joyful side. One man, with a strange grotesque gargoyle sort of face, who was more influenced by his love for me than by the deep spiritual change that had begun in the others, thinking that he would certainly be called upon to 'make a prayer,' had prepared himself beforehand for the emergency. He learned an oration by heart, or rather, in this instance, I should say by head, and came into my presence with it at full cock, warranted to go off at the least notice. So when two or three of the others had given vent to their few broken heartfelt utterances, he began with a flourish of Jewish trumpets, 'O Thou that dwellest between the cherubims!' There was a dead pause. Then turning his queer face over his shoulder, he said, with a piteous bleat to me, 'Oh, Miss, I'm stuck fast, I can't get on!'

Still on my knees, I solemnly answered, 'Never

mind, my brother, God will teach you another time;' and at once began a few words of concluding prayer. But alas for an unfortunately keen sense of the ridiculous! For a few moments my voice quivered and wavered on the very verge of laughter, and it was only by a superhuman effort that I managed to control myself. When I rose from my knees I felt as if my hair must have turned grey in the struggle.

Not many Sundays had passed before I noticed an old man who always sat in the same place, and listened to me with a queer, perplexed look on his weather-beaten face. I soon ascertained that he was popularly known by the name of 'Old Tom,' and was a well-sinker, who for seventy years had led a wild and desperate life; the hair-breadth escapes he had met with in his dangerous calling seeming only to have hardened him and made him more reckless. Time after time he had been dug out of the earth only to come up from his living grave to resume his wild courses. His only son had been struck dead before his eyes on the line; nothing seemed to make any impression on his hard old heart. But as he sat and heard for the first time of the love of his God; how the Father had never hardened His heart against His lost child; how the door of heaven was left on the latch even for such as he; how poor old Tom's very place was kept up in heaven 'prepared for him,' if only he would arise and come home to his Father, strange thoughts were stirred in that dim old mind. But poor old Tom had one difficulty, which always seemed to stand in the way. 'I'm no scholard,' he used to say to himself, scratching his grey head in a perplexed sort of way; 'it ain't no manner of use, I don't know how to make a prayer.'

At last he heard me give an account of how a working-man they all knew and respected came to be what he was. He was once a farm-servant in a Christian family, when the mother of the house died quite suddenly. The father sent for his two sons; and when they met, they fell on one another's necks and wept, and comforted one another with the words of ever-lasting life. And the young man felt how beautiful a thing is family love in Him in whom all the families of the earth are blessed, and turned away with a longing to be like that father and his two sons. He crept up into a hay-loft, and there and then, to use his own words, 'for the first time I knelt down and tried to pray. I didn't know a bit how, but somehow or other I managed to blunder on, and I blundered on that night and the next morning, till somehow,' he added, with a sudden smile, full of the peace of God, 'my blundering on found me my Saviour.'

'Well,' thought old Tom, and a gleam of light came into the dark perplexed face, 'I'm no scholard; I can't make a prayer, but I can blunder on.'

The next day he was sinking a well a hundred and twenty feet below the surface of the earth. His fellow-workmen had left him alone to finish his dangerous job. Suddenly all the words he had heard and all his sinful life came over him, and he felt he must pray there and then. So, kneeling down by the side of his old bucket, he put his rough, horny hands together, and, while the great tears streamed down that rugged face, he prayed his first prayer: 'O Lord, I'm the biggest of sinners, but you are a bigger Saviour. O Lord, save poor old Tom from his sins, and give him a new heart, for Jesus Christ's sake.' And at the bottom of that deep well, a hundred and twenty feet below the surface of the earth, the great Saviour and the great sinner met together, and when poor old Tom was pulled up to the surface he was a new creature in his God.

He came eleven miles away from his work, and waited four hours outside my house, to tell me of his conversion; and I had to take him in at eleven o'clock at night, when I got home, to give thanks to the Father for him.

Poor old Tom! he never saw me without asking me if I wanted a well sunk, that he would be glad to do it 'gracious' for me if I did. I believe he would gladly have bored the earth under my feet into a bottle-rack 'gracious,' if by so doing he could have testified the love and gladness of which his old heart was full.

Another of my regular attendants I noticed

always sitting close to me, with one hand up to his ear, listening with a look of rapt attention. I soon became acquainted with him, and found he was an intelligent and well-educated man, a gardener by trade, but placed in circumstances of great home unhappiness. His wife had formed a sort of maniacal hatred to him, which showed itself in persistent efforts to injure him, and alienate the hearts of his children from him. Always a moral man, he had resisted the temptation to drown his sorrow in intemperance, but he had never found any comfort in religion. He had tried church after church, but finding his deafness made it impossible for him to hear, he had latterly given up going to any place of worship, and had shut himself up in his miserable home. His heart was beginning to darken down into a reckless despair, when curiosity led him to the Abbey school-meeting, to see what it was like. To his surprise and delight he could hear my clear penetrating woman's voice with ease; and before two or three Sundays had passed, he had found the peace which passeth understanding in his

God, 'the place of rest imperturbable, where love is not forsaken if itself forsaketh not.' The whole expression of his face changed; he had the look of those

> . . . in this loud stunning tide
> Of human care and crime,
> With whom the melodies abide
> Of th' everlasting chime;
> Who carry music in their heart
> Thro' dusky lane and wrangling mart;"

and his love and gratitude found radiant expression in the lovely flowers with which he filled my drawing-room. His great natural beauty of character grew perfected by divine grace, and despite his deafness he became an earnest worker. A year or two after his wife became a Christian, and they were re-united in the love that passeth knowledge. For both I have had long since to give thanks as having departed in God's holy faith and fear.

The tokens of gratitude I received were of the most varied kinds, ranging, as may be seen, from the offer of a well to a gift of flowers. Fresh eggs, a chicken, a Bible, a hare—N.B. not poached—a Church Service, posies of all sorts and sizes, a cluster of field-birds shot at dawn, whose tender little loosened throats and filmy eyes I nearly wept over as I held them up by their pretty coral feet, but which nevertheless made an excellent pie, a small gold locket, etc., etc. On one occasion, two very tall heads of Brussel-sprouts were brought to the week-day meeting, and duly presented after it was over, when I disappeared in triumph with one under either arm, like a modern Daphne, sprouting cabbage instead of laurel, as befits this utilitarian age.

At times, however, in my day and night visiting among my rough people, my experiences were by no means so satisfactory, and often sharply taxed my mother wit how best to extricate myself from an awkward position. On one occasion, I found myself between a drunken husband and wife, in just that stage of inebriety which makes a man quarrel with his shadow for keeping close at his heels. Unfortunately this man was not reduced to his shadow, being well supplied with a substantial loud-tongued wife to exercise upon, and very soon they got to high words, drowning my feeble efforts to make myself heard. They were so maddening one another, that I saw in a very few moments they would come to blows, utterly regardless of my presence, and for all I could do to prevent it, he might half kill her under my eyes. What was to be done? My eyes fell on a tea-tray, with some loose cups and saucers and spoons upon it. In a moment I set to work, and hammered on it with such inspired energy, producing such a rattling fugue of cups and saucers and tea-tray, as effectually drowned the voices of my belligerents. For a few moments they tried to go on shouting at one another, but, bless you! it did no harm, as neither could hear the other, and soon they gave it up in despair.

Then I put in a few mild persuasive words, till they began at one another again; and again I betook myself to my loud but peaceful drum till I gained myself another short hearing. At last, between these 'two voices,' mine and the tea-tray's, I got them into a better frame of mind, and the threatened danger was averted.

On another occasion, a drunken tailor, whom his wife persisted in fetching out of a public-house for me to exhort, greatly embarrassed me by insisting on 'seeing me straight home,' as he expressed it, with a ludicrous disregard to facts, and the irregular curves and zig-zags we should infallibly describe in his present condition. However, as the choice lay between having him as my escort or leaving him to vent his ill-humour in beating his wife, I resigned myself to my fate. I believe I walked miles before I reached home that night. I never estimated before the force of the drunken Irishman's exclamation, on being condoled with on the length of way he had come, 'Och, yer honour, it's not the length but the breadth.'

My difficulties during the first few months of my work were further enhanced by a strong opposition from without. The unreasoning feeling against a woman fulfilling her Lord's injunction, 'Go tell My brethren that I go unto My Father and their Father, to My God and their God,' was stronger then than it is now. The old tendency to stick to the letter of

Scripture, and sin against its divine progressive spirit, to bind women, after nineteen centuries of freedom, with precisely the same bandages and restrictions which were necessary to preserve social order when first the equality of the sexes was practically assumed by Christianity, was then in full force. Nay, the usual tendency showed itself to extend these restrictions from their original use, as regulations for the *ecclesia*, the public and authorised services of the church, to all cases whatever; rendering it unlawful, not only for me to teach my poor, ignorant men, who were willing to be taught about God and Christ by me, and by no one else, but also for a mother to teach her grown-up sons, a queen to address her parliament, a woman to teach the public by her written words. A storm accordingly raged for some time against me, during which my own clergyman stood valiantly by me, quietly urging, on all sides, that some of the worst drunkards and blasphemers in his parish were now regular and consistent communicants at his church; was he to prefer their remaining drunkards and blas phemers to their being influenced by a lady, and oppose what God had blessed?

For some months the opposition lasted; but for the encouragement of all steady workers, I gladly record that, even in one of the great centres of ecclesiasticism, it gave way before good work and practical results. The leading Evangelical clergyman, who had begun by cutting me in the streets, ended by presenting me with four volumes of his sermons in token of his esteem and sympathy with my work. Being of a placable disposition I built the bulky tomes up into an altar of friendship in one corner of my room, and I need scarcely say that my sense of reverence forbade my ever disturbing the sacred stones.

But what I most needed never failed me—the support of my own clergyman, the friendship and hearty co-operation of one of our Indian missionaries, then working as a curate in the same district as myself, and, what was sweetest and best, the tender, wise sympathy of my father.

CHAPTER III.

INTELLECTUAL GOSPELS AND THE PEOPLE.

BUT how did I get this influence over working men? perhaps some one will ask, starting, as I did, with no knowledge of them as a class, or as individuals, and finding myself in a few weeks with some thousand on my hands. As the answer to this question may be helpful to other workers, I will try and reply to it in some detail.

The class I had to deal with were, with a slight admixture of fossil-diggers, answering in some respects to navvies, just the common artizans of any non-manufacturing town,—bricklayers, carpenters, shoemakers, gas-men, well-sinkers, farm labourers, etc. Wild as they were in their habits, I always say that for head and heart you could scarcely match them. Their ignorance, in its depth and solidity, to the last was a surprise to me; the learned pig would certainly have beaten them in a competitive examination; but at the same time they were possessed of a plenitude of mother wit, which made them a delightful, but difficult, audience to address. I remember one of the members for the University, himself a noted speaker, saying, that he would rather address any other mob; that if an accident did happen to one's nominative, or one's feet got hopelessly entangled in a broken construction, there was no hope of its passing unobserved,—the speaker's confusion was certain to be rendered worse confounded by a perfect storm of banter and rough jokes. The element of the clever, sceptical mechanic was wholly wanting. I only met with one case of intellectual doubt of the shallowest kind, a fervent disciple of Shelley; but there was a good deal of rough scepticism of a moral kind among them. The rooted belief in a good-natured, easy-going God, who would never be hard on a poor fellow whatever his life might be, and a consequent total disbelief in

His moral laws; a conviction that all religion was a sham; much Pharisaism in fustian that thanks God it is not as other men are; methodists, saints, cants, hypocrites; 'I give tithes of all I possess to the devil, and get fresh twice in the week;' a hatred of parsons; an ideal of manliness which aimed alternately at the beer barrel and the bull-dog; and a disbelief in punishment hereafter,—these were the chief enemies to be contended against, and I found them quite enough.

In the first place it was quite useless to preach ready-made doctrines to them. Justification by faith, imputed righteousness, vicarious satisfaction, election, sacramental grace, regeneration, —all these things were simple Greek to them. Perhaps it was fortunate that it was so; for at that time I was passing through the intellectual difficulties which most thoughtful young minds of the present day must encounter, and my hold on received opinions, except so far as I could work them out for myself, was loosened. It was evident that they and I must begin from the beginning.

I have often thought that if some of our great

thinkers could have my problem to solve, it would be a very good thing for them. If only once they could wake up one morning, and find themselves with some thousand rough but shrewd fellows on their hands to be *saved somehow*, saved in that grossly intelligible sense of the word salvation which even Mr. Voysey would accept —saved from sin and degradation. There they were; I could not get rid of them, waiting with their listening faces turned towards me; some intelligible theory of the universe I must give them to get them to square their lives in obedience to its laws. Would it be any use to tell them 'of a stream of tendency, not ourselves, which makes for righteousness?' Alas! the stream of tendency with which they were most familiar, made for the public-house and wife-beating. Or would it be any good to preach to them the 'method of Jesus,' the duty of self-abnegation, to these men who were driven, by every wild passion of their natures, to self-indulgence—passions that would make short work of any abstract notions, and could only be cast out by some other passion of love and adoration, such as only a living person can inspire? Or was I to follow Mr. Herbert Spencer, and rise with them from the lower to the higher religion, and preach to them the great inscrutable Power, to which neither personality nor emotion can be assigned, and expect that the knowledge of It would regulate their moral emotions, with which It was out of all relation? Or even preach a moral and beneficent Being, the Ruler of all things, far removed from them in the altitude of His perfections and blessedness; when the misery and disorder of their lives was a proof either that He did not mind, or if He did, didn't much care?

Alas! I felt forlornly enough that my intellectual gospels had but one fault when brought into contact with the mass of humanity—*they would not work.* The intellectual few might be saved; but as for this people that knoweth not, on this showing we must say, with the Pharisee of old, 'They are cursed.' Only in the Christianity of the Bible could I find what I wanted; could I not work out some simple form of it for them and me?

I took my stand at once on the great facts of life and conscience. I never laid any doctrine before them without first carefully verifying it for them from their own life, their own conscience, their own heart. If for one moment I departed from this ground, I felt at once I had lost my hold upon them. At one fell swoop I had to get rid of all petrified dogmas, and received opinions, and orthodox phraseology, and stick to what I could in some measure prove.

My first effort was to get them to believe in moral law; that there are great inevitable laws in the moral world as well as in the physical, and what a man sows that will he also reap. When they used to say to me, 'I don't believe in hell; God is much too merciful to damn a poor fellow like me,' I answered cheerfully, 'Of course He is much too good and merciful. It is not God that "damns you," as you say; it is you that condemn your own selves to a life of sin and misery away from Him.' And I used to illustrate it by what happened to Dr. Brown, the author of 'Rab and his Friends,' in the great cholera year. He was then a young man, practising at Chatham, when one night he was called up to go at once to a village down the Thames, where the cholera had broken out. The men rowed for their lives, for they were pulling against Death. The first thing he did after he had prescribed for the sick, was to call all who were not already stricken together. Not one would allow it, but he could see, by a look in their faces, that they were all in for the cholera. So he gave them a prescription which, he assured them, if taken in time, would save their lives. They all took it but one woman. In vain he entreated; she obstinately refused. 'She was not going to have the cholera—not she.' They all had it; but that woman was the only one who died of it. 'Now, then,' I asked, 'was it the doctor's fault?'

'No, that it warn't; it was the woman's own fault.'

'Well, then, you have got a disease in your soul called sin; you may deny it in words, but you know it; and, what's more, God knows it, and offers you a remedy. He offers you a Saviour, and He says to the heart that loves and receives Him, "The blood of Jesus Christ cleanseth from all sin." But you won't take the remedy, and you perish. Whose doing is it; God's or your own?'

'Well, I know I am in the wrong way now; but before I die I mean to turn over a new leaf.'

'You mean to say you will cry, "Lord, have mercy upon me" on your death-bed, and then you think you will be all right. My brother, be sure of this, there's no such thing as running up a bill all our lifetime with the devil, and then sneaking out when pay-time comes. You are much too honest yourself not to see that.'

Sometimes I used to put it differently to them. 'Well, suppose you were to go to Heaven, with your unchanged hearts, when you die, what would you do there? Death itself won't change you. Death is no more than birth. The child that is diseased before birth is diseased after birth. Would you be happy? What! no publics, no getting fresh, no loose talk and jolly songs, nothing but good things, the very mention of which makes you uncomfortable? Why, you would be like a man a friend of mine, a physician, was called in to see. He was a farmer, who had lived a bad life all his days, ruined his constitution by drinking, and now all the doctors in the world could not save him. So Dr. Bull said he had better send for a clergyman, and prepare himself for another world, as his days in this were numbered. The dying man accordingly turned to his wife, and asked her to send for their minister, when she burst out into a bitter laugh. "What," she exclaimed, "are *you* thinking of going to Heaven after all? And what will you do when you get there? You'll be like a pig in a parlour!" 'If it were possible to put a sinner into Heaven,' I used to urge, ' you could not put him in a hotter hell.'

And little by little they came to see the great Christian doctrine, that eternal sin must be, in the very nature of things, eternal punishment and eternal misery, and that salvation means being saved from the guilt and power of sin and selfishness, and not merely going to Heaven. As to the speculative point, whether moral evil is eternal, whether in that κόλασις αἰώνιος, the 'chastisement of ages,' into which the wicked are told to depart, there be ultimate purification and deliverance from the worm that dieth not and the fire that is not quenched, the remorse and the suffering that eternally cling to moral evil, I simply let that alone. It is with the chances of this world, and not of the next, that we are practically concerned.

But how to make them feel not only the consequences of sin, but what sin is in itself before God, its exceeding sinfulness, I frankly confess I found but one means for doing this— Christ and the Cross of Christ. In that perfect manhood, so tender yet so strong, courageous unto death for the truth; pitilessly severe against all sham and dishonesty, but opening its arms for the weary and heavy-laden to rest, and weep upon its breast; cutting keen as crystal through all false pretences, yet, like crystal, yielding to the weakest beam of light, and dyeing it with a thousand lovely hues, so that the repentant harlot becomes, under that gracious influence, a saint, and the rude fisherman an apostle of the world; in Him, taking our children in His arms, feeling for all human sorrow, weeping beside our open graves, healing all who were oppressed, they grew ashamed of their own low type of manhood. And in the suffering, the blood, the agony, the death of shame that the world's evil, that our sin cost the Son of God, they began to realise the exceeding hatefulness of sin; while in that God spared not His own Son, but freely gave Him up for us all, they were led to realise God's love to the sinner, the heart of their Father towards them. I troubled them with no theories, I simply gave them the facts; and I illustrated those facts, not by foolish figments about a good little boy bearing the punishment of a bad little boy, or an impossible monarch who caused himself to be flogged in the stead of his rebellious soldiers, but by all the most sweet and solemn facts of life. For whatever difficulties may be felt about the Atonement, the fact of it is woven into the very warp and woof of human life. Vicarious suffering meets us, pleading with pierced hands, at every turn. We could not enter into life but by the anguish of the One who loves us best. The innocent beasts must bleed and die that we may live. Our sin and sorrow is for ever pressing on the hearts of those that love us, and becoming their shame and their pain. Love crowned with our thorns is for ever atoning for us, putting away our selfishness, and making us 'at one' with our better selves. All human life is made up of fragments of the true Cross; and all things lead up to Him, who loves us with more than a mother's love, suffered for us more than a mother's pangs, bears with us with more than a mother's patience. And however men may dispute over the theory, the Atonement did become a great fact in our midst. Beneath the power of the Cross of Christ, I have seen four hundred rough, world-hardened, reckless men, weeping and sobbing like children over their sins. I have seen, Sunday after Sunday, bad men turned into good by it, men who were drunkards, profligates, blasphemers, fighters, gamblers, turned into good, devout, tender-hearted men. For months I never spoke but this change took place, two or three thus receiving the word of life, and becoming completely changed men. How then can Christianity be anything but a great life-giving fact to me?

One man in particular, I remember, so wild a fellow that on taking his wages, he would sometimes drink all Saturday night and Sunday, and return to his work on the Monday morning, never having set eyes on his starving wife and children, and having spent all the money which ought to have gone to their support. He came into the Abbey school-room a drunken blasphemer; he left it a Christian man. His own simple account of his sudden conversion was, 'I heard that my Saviour lived and died for me; now I mean to live and die for Him.' That man, with all that force of evil habit in him, never had a fall. I always think the happiest moment of my life was one summer evening when I went into his cottage. His wife was out, but through the staircase door that stood open, I could hear him praying with his little child, as he put her to bed, the child's soft voice following his as they trod that homeward path together. A few moments after he appeared in his working dress, just as he had come off the brickfields, with the peace of God shining in his face.

But with these terrible struggles with evil going on all around me, with some so bound and tied with the chain of their sins that, though they heard my voice and would fling themselves down on their knees at my side, they seemed powerless to break loose from the force of evil habit; nay, by my own need of courage and wisdom, and my own deep consciousness of its being given in answer to prayer, I was literally driven to the belief in a great spiritual force, call it the Holy Spirit, or what you will, a divine energizing power which we can lay hold of by faith and make our own. More and more I taught them that conversion is a gift from God, to be had for the earnest asking; that the love of God is poured out (ἐκκέχυται) of His deep heart into ours by the Holy Spirit which is given us; and if they would only surrender themselves wholly to that mighty influence, they had but to open the door of their hearts, and that eternal sunshine would stream in;

while, without Him, all my talking to them was only so much physic poured down a dead man's throat.

And so they and I together worked out a simple theology for ourselves—faith in a Father in heaven, who loves us; in the cross of Christ, revealing the sinfulness of sin, and the love of God to the sinner, and the inmost meaning of which is death unto sin and life unto God; faith in a divine energizing Spirit; a recognition that, as long as we continue in a state of sin and selfishness, we are and must be in a state of punishment here and hereafter: and a belief in our Father's home where sin and sorrow would never enter. And for all practical purposes we found this simple faith enough.

CHAPTER IV.

MEN AND WOMEN.

IT must not be supposed that my work lay only among the men. In many ways I worked quite as hard among the women. Indeed, I am much disposed to agree with a well-known working-man political speaker, who, when I was suggesting carrying out some plan of reform by the help of men alone, exclaimed, 'Miss, you will do nothing without our female brethren. One female is worth ten males.' The women having chiefly the training of the rising generation, the man being out at work all day, her influence is necessarily the most important. But I confess that my whole experience has been that the best way to get at the women is to get at the men first, to recognise in this, as in other things, the Divine order that the man is the head of the woman, and while her head goes one way, it is very hard for the rest of her to go another; whilst her husband goes to the public-house and gets drunk, it is very hard for her to go to church and get pious. Indeed, I know no greater proof that with God all things are possible, than a drunkard's wife who is a Christian. But when the husband turned round, it was the exception, and not the rule, when the wife did not become earnest-minded as well.

My right-hand woman, to whom I always went for comfort and counsel in difficulties, was a certain old charwoman of the name of Phœbe Simpson. I should be loth that any notes of my work should go forth without embalming her precious old memory; like some sweet hedgerow flower laid between the leaves, dim with common dust, and yet touched with a beauty of the skies. I can see her now,—the short thick-set figure, the queer gentle old face, deeply lined with suffering and sorrow, the writing of God's finger, which I never see on an old face without a feeling of reverential awe; and looking out from the midst of it all, the dear old faded eyes, that seemed to have wept themselves dim with tears of pity. How much 'sweetness and light' lay hid behind that dress of rusty widow's black; what practical wisdom, what deep womanly compassions, linking the Divine with the human; what kindly humour, above all, what extraordinary moral and spiritual elevation! As long as Christianity can embody itself in Phœbe Simpsons, I can't help thinking it must be taken as its own evidence, and, in this solid form at least, can defy our modern critical acids.

Odd to say, Phœbe Simpson began her life in Christ in a thunderstorm,—one of the most terrible hail storms I believe on record having burst over the eastern counties; thinking the end of the world had come and found her in her sins, she knelt down and cast herself on her Saviour's love. The storm passed, but the love remained. How Phœbe Simpson got rid of her gossiping neighbours, and took up her neglected home duties, was most characteristic.

'How did you manage, Mrs. Simpson?' I once asked. 'For you know the Bible tells us to be courteous; and to turn folk out of our house, however much in the way they may be, is apt to look very rude.'

'I'll tell you how I managed that,' she answered, with the funny humorous twinkle that used to light up her quaint old face. ' The first thing I did was to get the brush and dust-pan and lay them handy 'gainst any neighbour comed in. Soon, in pops Mrs. Smith. 'Mrs. Smith,' says I, 'you won't mind my doing a bit of dustin', will you, whilst you're talkin'?' Of course she couldn't but be agreeable to that. So down on my knees I goes, and begins to dust with all my might. But somehow, it was a very curious thing, but the dust allus would gather thickest just under the chair my neighbour was a-sittin' on. She'd shift, and shift; but I'd allus be arter her with my old dust-pan, and the dust 'ud get up her nose, and she'd begin to sneeze ever so—ketcher! ketcher!—and soon she'd say, "Well, I think—ketcher!—I'll call in another day, Mrs. Simpson, as I see you are — ketcher! — busy." And so in less than a week I had dusted all my neighbours out of my house.'

Dear old Phœbe Simpson! she had a great

objection to the running tongue which so often goes with falling feet. I often think of her definition of religion, 'I think, Miss, religion is doing things still.' The words might be taken in their double sense, not only of that quietness and confidence which was so emphatically dear old Phœbe Simpson's strength, but of unweariedness in well-doing. Like a star, she was always about her silent tasks of light. Wherever there was a sore heart to be comforted, or a sore hand to be leeched or poulticed, among the neighbours round, you might be sure that Phœbe Simpson had been there before you. But to see her in her glory, one ought to see her in the ragged Sunday class of little waifs and strays she had gathered about her, carolling like a hoarse old lark at the top of her ancient voice, and followed by a rabble of childish pipes and trebles, which 'wandered on as loth to die,' without quite the sweetness of Wordsworth's echo, while she occasionally applied the well-worn corners of her hymn-book to a curly head that was not conducting itself with due propriety. I often wonder whether the present thriving Sunday-schools remember or even know of their humble parentage, the sweet old heart that out of the depth of her poverty, and the riches of her love, gave them birth in the cottage room in Gas Lane.

She was a much tried woman, plenteousness of tears to drink was her portion. 'Whom I tenderly love,* I rebuke and chasten.' Her only son was a great trouble to her. I can see him now, a great stalwart-looking fellow, but with a constitution utterly broken down by his wild drinking ways, pacing up and down my dining-room, exclaiming in agony,—

'They call it pleasure. But look at me, a young fellow of twenty-four, broken down with grinding like an old blind hoss in the devil's mill. They call it pleasure, but I call it hard work.'

I do not know whether his mother's prayers have yet been heard for him, but I only know with the Bishop of old, that the child of such prayers and tears cannot be lost.

* The word used here for love is not the ordinary word ἀγαπάω, but the more familiar word φιλέω used for the intimate love between two friends.

Dear old Phœbe worked with me heart and soul, in recruiting for my working-men's meetings. She would trot round from door to door to tell them I had returned from my summer holiday, and the meeting would be held as usual next Sunday, generally, however, being greeted with, 'We knowed that afore, missus. All right, we're a-coming.' The missionary earnestness, however, which the men inspired in her breast, and that of some other women, was not founded I fear on any high appreciation of the sex. I fear the value attached to the nobler male was decidedly low, and that the estimation in which he was held was pretty much expressed in the response I met with at one door, at which I had timidly knocked, to know if there were any men there I could ask to my meeting. 'No, thank God,' the woman replied, 'we have no males here;' and the door was banged in my face with a sharp snap, that gave a singular emphasis to the thanksgiving.

One of my great difficulties at first was one which I suppose all educated people feel,—how to put my thoughts into an effective and telling form, how, in one word, to speak to the people.

It is a mistake to suppose that plain and suitable commonplaces will go down with working-men. Working-men emphatically want strong meat, thoughts as racy as their own expressions; they reject sweet pap fit for children. But if any one supposes that my power of speaking to them was a gift that came naturally to me, without any effort on my part, let them, once for all, dispossess themselves of any such idea. Gift, like genius, I often think, only means an infinite capacity for taking pains. I served a hard apprenticeship enough. My familiarity with Shakespeare, Wordsworth, and Tennyson had fortunately trained me in the use of good Saxon English; I could speak of 'going to bed,' without saying, 'ere you resign yourself to repose.' But how to put things forcibly and clearly to uneducated men I set to work to learn from those who had proved themselves masters in the art; I carefully studied Spurgeon's sermons, and any other preacher to the people I could hear of; and I read many of the old Puritan writers, such as old Gurnall's 'Christian's Complete Armour,' Brooks, and writers even as late as Berridge, all of them remarkable for Shakespearian force and quaintness of expression; and I diligently wrote out any thought that might be useful to me, transforming and adapting it for my own purposes. I ransacked magazines, sermons, books of all kinds, for good, strong illustrations, which we must always remember are, to the mind of the uneducated, what diagrams and pictures are to the eye, explaining and embodying the meaning. Often as not, my own work gave me the best illustrations. I would take the next Sunday some difficulty or objection which had been suggested to me in conversation with some of the men during the week, and discuss its bearings for the good of all. When put before them, not as an abstract truth, but in the form of a talk with one of themselves, it came home to them with far more power.

Some of the compliments my speaking received were very funny. A farmer being asked what he thought of an address I had given, exclaimed, 'Why, I had no idea a woman could speak like that! It wasn't only what she said, it was the noise she made. It was splendid both ways!'

But what I found still more trying, were the wild renderings and transformations my words underwent at the hands of my audience. One dear old man, who, at the ripe age of seventy-eight, became an humble child-like Christian, and who twice in the week used to walk eight miles to hear me, had one favourite version of the words which caused his conversion, to which he adhered with frightful fixity, and retailed to every one he met. 'There was three of us old men a-settin' together, and you turned, and you shook your little finger at us, and you said: "You old men there, you are goin' to hell as fast as your old legs can carry you!" I never felt so afeard in my life, and I have been a changed man ever since.' Be it known, gentle reader, I am naturally reverent of age, and the utmost I could remember saying was, that I hoped that as their heads whitened, their faith brightened, and as all else grew dim to their old eyes, their Saviour's face and their Father's home grew clearer; so I can only suppose it was the strength of the impression I made which clothed itself in such terrific words.

A lady friend of mine who had won the next place in his heart to myself, greatly delighted him by presenting him with her photograph. He came in from the neighbouring village, where his small farm was situated, to tell me that he had had it framed: 'And I've hoonged her up next Mr. Spurgin; and the neighbours they come in and they say, "Well, they *du* look beautiful!"'

This same friend of mine was the only one, after they had lost their first friend, the clergyman's wife, who at all took her place by my side in their affections, and who on the rare occasions she could leave her own work to take mine, managed to speak home to their inmost hearts. 'You see, Miss, her words do weigh so heavy on the system,' as a working-man said to me. One young man, a wild, thoughtless fellow, became entirely changed under her influence, and his sister exclaimed to her, with earnest thankfulness, 'There's our Jem, he didn't even believe in the devil. But oh, Miss, he *do* believe in him now since he has heard you preach him.' If there was a weak point in my friend's theology, I fear it was the personality of the evil spirit, so the assurance was doubly satisfactory to her.

We both met with the most curious instances of the way in which, as in ancient prophesying, we were able to 'make manifest the secrets' of the hearts before us. On one occasion my friend said, 'There are some of you young men who think so lightly of coming into the presence of your God in this meeting, that as you stood outside the door you actually tossed up whether you would come in here or go to yonder public.' A group of young men sitting right in front of her, and who had come in late, had actually done so, and received the ghostly guidance of 'tails' to decide them to hear the gospel in preference to drinking in the public-house. On another occasion, I said, 'There are you men out there;'—pointing in their direction,—'you know you have been sitting in the public-house drinking up to the last moment. And one of you looked up at the public-house clock, and said, "Come, let's be off to hear the lady preach, or we sha'n't get a seat."' Without knowing it, I described a scene which had really taken place, and the man who had pointed to the clock and uttered the identical words, was so impressed at being thus 'judged of all,' that he became from that day an earnest-hearted man. At times it produced no small awkwardness; a man would go to another, and accuse him in great wrath of having told the lady all about him; and I had to step in and clear the supposed tale-bearer with the assurance that he had never mentioned the other's name.

But I soon found that you can make but very little way with ignorant minds by mere preaching. The 'after meeting,' which has since grown so common, to which those who were impressed might be asked to stay, and in which you could sit down on a bench by some poor ignorant fellow's side, and patiently get at his inarticulate difficulties and sorrows, and talk to him in plain brotherly fashion, became a necessity. As many as two hundred used sometimes to stay behind. We used to open it by prayer, in which those who were anxious to lead a new life were encouraged to make their first confession of faith to their Father and their Saviour. It was difficult at times to prevent an inward smile at the quaint simplicity of their expressions; and I remember my heart being refreshed, but my gravity somewhat tried, by the fervency with which one man prayed, 'O Lord, bless this here woman what preaches.' Prayer being concluded, the whole meeting broke up into groups of earnest talkers. Here again you must depend on the number and earnestness of your helpers, earnest working-men and women being especially useful in this part of the work, from the fact of their having overcome the same difficulties and temptations as those they address. Many a fleeting impression was riveted for time and eternity, by being taken hold of at once in the after meeting, and stamped in by earnest brotherly talk and prayer.

The choice of door-keepers too is very important. I chose out two of the most gentlemanly and good-looking of the earnest working-men for this office; and I was often amused at the air with which they handed some poor ragged object, fresh from the public-house, to his seat, with as much deference as if he had been the Archbishop of Canterbury himself. We may smile, but a respectful welcome is never lost on the sensitive pride of working-men.

By degrees I was also led to feel the absolute necessity of some social reforms for any widespread good to be effected. 'It's nothing of a trade since this here woman has been preaching,' a publican lamented to a policeman. But all the more strongly I felt the need of some substitute for the public-house. We too often forget that men in that rank of life, however much attached to their homes, require the society of their fellows as much as men in our own rank, some place in which they can see the newspapers, and talk trade and politics. Their own homes are too small to allow of their seeing their friends in them as we do; and while the public-house formed a strong public opinion on the side of evil, I saw the men who had been influenced for good reduced to pious units in the narrow circle of their own homes. So by my dear father's influence, and by his giving his scanty leisure from scientific pursuits to the labour of raising funds, a Working-men's Club and Institute was built, and has since proved very successful, and is in itself a protest against prevailing intemperance.

It is unnecessary for me to enter into the causes which laid me aside after two or three years in an illness which lasted many years, causes, however, which had nothing to do with overwork; or to touch on the reasons which have since reluctantly obliged me to take up other work—work not of my own choice, but which I feel has a greater claim on me as a woman.*

Though no one was found exactly to take up my work, I learnt that God 'fulfils Himself in many ways.' Earnest men and women have devoted their lives to those back streets and lanes and alleys; and the suburb where I laboured has realized the wish of an Irish speaker, embodied in an irresistible pun, that

* See 'Work in Brighton;' with a Preface by Florence Nightingale. Twelfth Edition. Price 6d. (Hatchards.)

Barnwell might soon become Barnbetter. For many of my dear friends it has become too respectable, and they have moved on to another suburb; thus awaking in my mind the old difficulty which has always troubled me at times, why the world is round. If it had only a brink, so that we might be always improving the hopeless ones in the rear, pushing them on gently but irresistibly, till if they positively refused to be bettered, we might improve them over the edge, out of a world which no longer wants them. As it is we too often push our worst snail over into our neighbour's garden.

But even in this sphere that has no limiting sides to it perhaps we gain the best image of that Love which has no end, the love of the Cross, 'whose breadth is charity, whose length is eternity, whose height is omnipotence, and whose depth is unsearchable wisdom.'

CHAPTER V.

EVANGELIZATION.

LET me now dwell a little more generally on some social questions which especially affect the welfare of the working classes, as well as enter a little more in detail on the best general means of getting hold of what Dr. Chalmers used to call the 'lapsed classes,' the masses of working-men and women who, in the expressive elliptical phrase that has coined itself for the occasion, 'go nowhere.'

In dealing with the religious difficulty, the fact that so many working-men go to no place of worship, and are in no vital union with any section of the Christian Church, of course I shall be met at the outset with the current objection of comfortable middle-class worshippers, that there are plenty of churches and chapels open now-a-days, that these people live within the sound of church bells, and if they go nowhere it is their own fault.

There is a little paper of Nathanael Hawthorne's, in which he points out to us the immense improvements this age of mechanical inventions has introduced into the journey to the Celestial City since Bunyan's day. Where the original wicket gate stood, now stands a commodious station, where each pilgrim takes his ticket, labelled Anglican, Methodist, Baptist, etc., according to the line he travels on, the Slough of Despond having been long ago filled in with German Rationalism and French novels, and bridged over by modern science, for the Celestial 'Bus to pass to and fro; Apollyon's services have been engaged as stoker and engine-driver; and we have tunnelled through the Hill Difficulty and filled up the Valley of Humiliation with the debris; only, unfortunately, quite at the last the writer's mind is darkened with a doubt whether the destination is quite the same, whether, after all, we shall not find ourselves at the wrong place. But it strikes me that we have introduced modern improvements into the parable of the Good Samaritan, as well as into Bunyan's dear old-fashioned allegory, of quite as fatal, though of a less extensive kind. The 'Good Samaritan' has no need to get off his beast now-a-days, and go to the wounded man 'where he is;' least of all to go to the sensational length of giving up his own beast to him, and himself trudging laboriously on foot; he contents himself with the reflection that the inn is close by where he can get attended to, and it is his own fault if he doesn't go to it. He needn't trouble himself any longer with the question whether, as he is half-dead, he isn't too far gone to care, or to get there, if he did care; but rides on, with the comfortable reflection that so much is being done for people of his class. Only, in this version of the parable, one cannot help asking whether the Samaritan has not reverted to the older and commoner type of his race, those 'who feared the Lord, *and* served their own idols.'

" Is it the fault of the bed-ridden cripple that

he does not get up and go to the doctor who lives close by; or is it the doctor's fault who leaves him to perish by refusing to go to him? Is it not just the malady of the people who, perhaps, live in the next street to us, that their wills *are* bed-ridden, that they cannot rise and come, however many churches we may open for them? Is it not just this that constitutes their claim to our help? And if much is done for them, before we can rest satisfied, does not the further question remain, Is it done rightly? Is it done with a full understanding of their needs and with the hearty human fellowship and sympathy of man to man?

For I go one step further. Are our Church services adapted to them, if they did come? 'What,' says Edward Denison, who went and lived among the working people in the East End of London,—'what is the use of telling people to come to church when they know of no rational reason why they should; when, if they go, they find themselves among people using forms of words which have never been explained to them; ceremonies performed which, to them, are entirely without meaning; sermons preached which, as often as not, have no meaning, or, when they have, a meaning intelligible only to those who have studied religion all their lives?'*

To us, who from our earliest childhood have been familiar with the Church prayers, no service can have quite the same hallowed charm. The venerable forms, the occasional obsolete words, the archaic modes of expression, are all to us like old cathedral stones that bear the weather-stains of centuries, and the swallow's nest of yesterday, beautiful with the sorrows and adorations of the past, yet from whence the fresh aspirations of to-day take heavenward flight. But do we realise the difficulties they may present to uneducated minds, to whom they are unfamiliar and unhallowed by association? I remember having this forcibly brought home to me by a working-man who became an earnest Christian through my mission services. This man had not been in any place of worship for

* Letters and Other Writings of the late Edward Denison, p. 39.

eighteen years,—I do not mention it as anything particularly unusual,—but as soon as he had got a decent suit of clothes he went to the parish church. From his first church-going he came away in a state of the profoundest bewilderment, and going straight to a friend of mine, he asked her, 'Ma'am, what *is* that we says in church when we all bow our 'eads? Who was that feller, Pontius Pilate, who went down into 'ell? and I did think when a chap once went there he never comed up again the third day.' Yet this man was an intelligent fellow enough, only give him time to rub off the rust of his wild and uncared-for life; and, though I don't think he ever got over the moral shock of that unlooked-for coming up of Pontius Pilate from the place of perdition, or took to the Church service after it, he certainly became a thoughtful and consistent member of a chapel.

But apart from our Church service not being adapted for a Mission-service, the great clothes difficulty will always block the way in any regular church or chapel with a well-clad middle-class congregation.* The ordinary working-man, who goes to no place of worship, has, generally speaking, no suit of 'Sunday best;' often enough he has only 'the clothes he stands upright in;' not infrequently, in his own expressive vernacular, he has drunk the shirt off his back, and it is simply impossible to get him at once to form part of a well-dressed congregation. He feels himself a fustian patch on all that silk and broad-cloth. The difficulty presses heavily enough on even a Mission-service, without any need to add to it; and long ago, had my sex permitted it, it would have reduced me to acting on the energetic utterance of a minister at the London Conference of clergy and working-men, 'If it is clothes that are your difficulty, I will preach the gospel to you in my shirt-sleeves any day.' It even evolves itself out of one's very success; what the connexion between

* It must be understood that, in these papers, I am speaking of the lower substratum of working-men, such as exist in every town, not of respectable mechanics, nor of the large and increasing body of total abstainers,—a great proportion of whom are absorbed in various Christian denominations.

Christianity and broad-cloth is I know not, it is hidden in the mystery which besets the *causal nexus* in general; but it must be a vital one. In my own Mission-service conversion was always marked by a suit of black. And nothing but the excessive crowding, which hid all individual shortcomings, especially about the nether man, kept the dread of my heart from being realised, of growing too respectable.

Such being the difficulties to be overcome, if ever the Church is to regain her lost ground with the people, it can only be by having some simpler shorter service especially adapted to their wants, and forming a nursery-ground for both church and chapel. Let them be planted down at regular intervals in the poorer neighbourhoods, and held in school-rooms or any large-enough room that offers itself. Let each parish or congregation have its Mission-service —as much part of its regular machinery as its district-visiting, its Sunday-schools, its Bible-classes, etc.—and let it be as carefully organised and worked; and we should soon see a marked change for the better in our people. Those who are aware of the remarkable work of evangelization that is going on in Paris among the working-classes by means of small earnest gatherings, held in almost every street, in the face of all the difficulties presented by Roman Catholicism, the religious apathy of the people, and the law that forbids the assembling together for Protestant worship of more than twenty people, know all that may be effected by this agency if made an earnest and thorough use of, and not treated in the slipshod manner it too often is.

The service must be held on Sunday. Weekday services are little or no use for purposes of evangelization. The very men who want it most, the careless and indifferent, are much too tired after their day's work to care to come to a religious service, which has no attractions for them. And, besides, so unusual a proceeding exposes them to being unmercifully 'chaffed,' and therefore requires extra moral courage. It should be held on Sunday evening,—not the afternoon, when the men often lie down and have a sleep,—or at any rate not earlier than half-past three. And it should not be reduced, as mine was, to an inconvenient hour from fear of interfering with church hours. Church hours are not interfered with in the case of those who never go to church. We have made our 'church hours' Molochs long enough, to which the souls of our people have been sacrificed. The service itself may consist of the General Confession, Thanksgiving, and Lord's Prayer—three hymns, if possible with choruses for those who can't read to follow, a very few verses of the Bible, not a whole chapter—an address, and a short extemporary prayer, the whole lasting not more than an hour. Everything should be short, prompt, and hearty, with no dragging, and plenty of variety.

And now as to the speaking, the most important point, and always the difficult one.

In the first place it must be good, simple, hearty, and to the point. The Mission-service must not be trusted to the first raw curate or earnest lay stick who offers—men to whom the incumbent of the parish would never think of entrusting his own pulpit, knowing that he would empty his church if he did. The clergy must disabuse themselves once for all of the idea that anything will do for these poor people—they are so ignorant. Anything will *not* do for workingmen. The more ignorant they are, the less accustomed to religious forms of speech, the better speaking they require, the greater the art needed in the speaker to address them effectively. Suitable commonplaces will emphatically not go down with them. They require good strong racy speaking, and, above all, stamped with the utmost reality—no fighting with 'extinct Satans,' no religious phraseology, no fossilized dogmas. The brawny blacksmith who, wrestling in prayer, and much perplexed in heart at the strength of evil, cried out, ' O Lord, the devil *is* so strong; but Thou art stronger; knock him down, O Lord! O Lord, in Thy great goodness, knock him down!' is no bad type of the earnestness and directness and straight-hitting a speaker to working-men needs, that speaking out of the heart and the life, to which they never fail to respond.

Only, as old Gurnall says, he must not be 'fed with a spoon too large to go in at his mouth,' with long words which he cannot possibly understand.

It is a curious and most uncomfortable anomaly that the language chosen to convey eternal realities is the most unreal and Latinised language there is,—language in which it would never occur to us to address one we love, or obtain the necessaries of existence, or do any of the real work of life. Pulpit English is the most vicious English in existence. I have myself heard a clergyman instinctively do into Latin the Saxon account of the Demoniac in St. Mark, 'There met Him a man coming out of the tombs,' which in the course of his remarks he rendered, 'They were immediately encountered by an individual proceeding from the tombs;' and I have heard another clergyman inform his congregation of village clodhoppers that 'our Lord did not indulge in nugatory predictions,' by way of bringing home to them that He is the faithful and true. During the Irish famine, the shifts the clergy were reduced to to avoid any indecorous mention of the potato in the pulpit were curious, though why a potato should be more profane than the 'hyssop on the wall' I cannot conceive, since the same God made them both. Some called it 'the succulent esculent;' others alluded distantly to it as 'that useful edible which forms so important a staple of food;' while only one Irish clergyman was found who, in a kind of Celtic reaction, courageously informed his congregation that their contributions had provided thirty starving families with 'good Irish stoo.'

Now, cannot we speak to the people in the English in which Tennyson and Wordsworth write? Does it show any real culture to say, 'Ere you resign yourself to repose,' instead of 'Before you go to bed'? Cannot we call a spade a spade, and not 'an agricultural instrument'? Not so very long ago I heard an address in a Mission-service of the very poorest, from a speaker appointed by a clergyman, which began thus: 'The note, my fellow-townsmen, I mean to strike to-night is one of expostulation,' and the discourse went on to allude to the transit of Venus, which the people probably set down as some new kind of cheese, or the last superfine tea,—the worthy speaker was a grocer by worldly calling,—and ended with a good thick layer of doctrine, which might have been living at some remote geological period, probably before man had made his appearance on the earth, but which so far as having any vital connexion with heart, life, or conscience might have been dug out of the old red sandstone. As the long words rolled out, I was irresistibly reminded of a medical man in the north who was noted for his Johnsonian English. Having on one occasion to prescribe for a dying labourer, he sent him a draught, labelled 'to be taken in a recumbent posture.' As to what this might be the relatives of the dying man were utterly at fault. They sent over to the linen-draper, to know if he had a recumbent posture. No, he had never heard of such a thing. Perhaps it might be something in the bladder line. Did the butcher chance to have one? No, he had never heard of such a thing either. At last, they worked their way round to an old woman, who never would allow herself at fault in anything. So she said, 'Yes, she had one; but, most unfortunately, she had just lent it!'

Now, my one advice to speakers at Mission-services is, like the old woman, to lend or sell their 'recumbent postures,' and speak good plain English. And if good effective speaking does not come to them by nature, like Dogberry's reading and writing, why not study those who are masters of the art, the well-known preachers of the day, who have gained the ear of the people? Why not read some of the old Puritan writers—Gurnall, Brooks, Flavel, etc.—for racy, powerful thoughts, or Spurgeon's 'Commentary on the Psalms,' especially prepared for village preachers, or Eugene Stock's 'Lessons on the Life of our Lord.'

Perhaps you say you don't like the theology of the old Puritans or Spurgeon. What does that matter? You may equally learn from their way of putting things; you may borrow their pitcher, even though you may fill it higher up the stream where you think the water flows clearer. Good speaking needs learning, at least as much as making shoes. And if some good folk are inclined to say, 'God does not want our learning,' still less, I would urge, does He want our laziness. If the Divine fire must come from above,—and no one can lay more stress than I do that spiritual power is essentially supernatural, and must be won by prayer and self-surrender to God,—yet the fuel must come from below, not without much digging and hewing.

I believe that one reason why working-men, as a rule, prefer the speaking of ladies, why they can always be got hold of at least in some measure by that agency when all others have failed, is in part that women never wrong their thoughts with pulpit English, but preserve the strength and sweetness of their mother tongue; and that they speak not from theological systems, but from the heart and the life, and from that deep understanding of the wants of the people, which comes from close and loving contact of their woman's heart with theirs.

But till we learn like our Master to give the working-men our best, and not merely the leavings of our middle-class congregations, till we carefully search out the best speakers for the Mission-service, without regard to the possibility of the susceptibilities of excellent Mr. Dryasdust

EVANGELIZATION. 79

being wounded by his being passed over,—in one word, till the good of the working-men becomes our *first* thought, they will never be won, the Mission-service will consist, as it so often does, of a few harmless old women; and those ribs of death, empty benches, will everywhere protrude to prove that it is not a living thing.

Good speaking alone, however, is not enough. A Mission-service, to be effective, as I have already said, should be carefully organized, else the best speaker is only a head without limbs. Not only does it need a body of earnest helpers to create an atmosphere of prayer and fervour, as well as to follow up any who are impressed, either at the after-meeting or at their own homes, but the task of bringing the people in ought to belong to them. The Mission-service has fortunately no church bells to whose cold iron throats we can depute the work of saying 'Come,' till we almost forget how to say it with our tender human throats, beneath which beats a human heart. The district visitors and a certain number of earnest working-men and women should meet their clergyman once a month in connexion with the Mission-service, for the appointment of speakers,—if there be no one effective speaker who will undertake it,—for the apportioning of work, for hearing of any cases that need his own visitation, and for earnest prayer. The district visitors should be required to know and report what men and women in their district go to no place of worship, and, if possible, to see them personally, and earnestly invite them to the Mission-service, not merely leaving a message for the man through his wife, which is of no manner of use. And the back streets should be apportioned among men and women who will undertake to go round on the Sunday before the service and personally ask the people to come, promising to be there to meet them, and give them a welcoming smile; and, in the case of some poor shy and reluctant fellows, to call for them and go with them. Many a man will be too shy to come alone, who will gladly come with another. I used to tell my working-men, 'Don't stick your arm out like a sign-post, and point a poor fellow to the meeting; your arm and mine has got this bend at the elbow, on purpose that it may bring our lost brother to Christ, link itself lovingly in with his in true brotherly fashion, and set him to come along with us.' The streets should be constantly interchanged at the monthly meeting, so that the invitation may come from a fresh voice. An illustrated leaflet, with an invitation to the meeting printed in red ink across the letter-press, forms a good excuse for knocking at the door and asking the people to come.

The terrible obstacle to the effective working of this vital part of a Mission-service lies in that curious anomaly which is eating out the heart of our middle-class Christianity,—religious selfishness. So far from our being willing to lay down our lives for the brethren, we are often not willing to lay down so much as one religious service, to give up one meal out of many for the sake of those who are perishing with hunger so, while the church is crowded, the Mission-service is too often left with only one or two to help it with their presence and their prayers. Here, alas! is, I fear, the root of the sterility of much of our Christianity.

But in the difficult work of getting at those

who are untouched by church or chapel we must not trust to any one agency. No one thing will do the work. Fresh agencies must always be coming in and taking the place of those that are getting worn out through the deadening influence of habit.

An earnest letter from the clergyman of the parish, or from the habitual speaker at the Mission-service, printed, but enclosed in an envelope,—for the poor are particularly sensitive to any little mark of respect and individual consideration,—left at every door at the beginning of the winter's work, will often bring many, and is also a source of communication between clergy and people.

Singing hymns in procession, if it be well and reverently done, and not so as to obstruct the more public thoroughfares when the authorities may object, forms a sweet and musical peal of church bells to call the people in. No one knows the full beauty of that grand old hymn,—

> 'Onward, Christian soldiers—onward,
> Marching as to war,'

till they have pealed it out under the winter stars.

But one of the most effective, yet I must

confess the most disagreeable way of getting at the lowest substratum, which must always be the aim and end of a Mission-service, is Saturday evening public-house visitation. It was the only part of my work to which I never could overcome my intense repugnance; but I would urge it on any one who is endeavouring to reach our home heathen. I used to do it in company with another lady every Saturday evening, devoting an hour and a half to it, from six to half-past seven; later than eight o'clock it would not be safe for ladies,—alas that it should be so in a Christian and civilized land!—besides being of no use, that terrible law of reversion to the original type—if we are to accept Mr. Darwin's theories of the descent of man—which obtains in the public-house, having taken place at any later hour, the man having gone back to the larger short-tailed ape, from which according to the great naturalist he originally sprang, deprived of God's great gift of speech and reason. But even at the earlier hour we chose, it was by no means pleasant. We used to call it going to evening service; the men are generally in that initial stage of drunkenness which makes a man awfully religious. The sermons I have had preached to me in the public-house, and always on the two texts, the shortness of human life and the necessity of serving God! It is not pleasant work, but speaking from my own wide experience, I can only positively say that ladies may trust working-men not to insult them under any circumstances, if they are making an effort for their good. I cannot quite promise for the publicans, as probably they do not consider it an effort for *their* good; but I must say as often as not I have found them most civil and polite. But even when the contrary, if it is sharp work, it is also short. One need only stay long enough to give out a few papers, with an earnest invitation to the meeting. But the mere sense that any one loves them and cares about them enough to come like the good Samaritan 'where they are' works wonders, and makes them think that there must be something in it after all. 'Blow'd if I don't come and see what it is like for myself,' as a working-man said in answer to one of my invitations.

A free tea might be given once a year to the men who, being out at work all day, and altogether removed from contact with clergy or district visitor, cannot be got at otherwise,— a free tea, with much hymn-singing of a loud cheerful sort, and plenty of good strong speaking of a kind that remembers Sydney Smith's warning, that 'sin is not got out of a man, as Eve was out of Adam, by casting him into a deep sleep;' not a dreary set-out of funereal meats, with which our people are too often regaled, but hearty, humorous speaking, that is not afraid of shaking off a man's stolid indifference by a good laugh, leaving him twice as ready to receive the graver truths, to gain an entrance for which must be the speaker's real aim,—speaking which can hide a good deal of straight hitting under a racy humorous saying. I can remember once, however, hitting a little too hard. I had been extremely annoyed at the bestial behaviour in the public-house of some of the drinking men who, I knew, were present; and having spoken with much warmth of my love for working-men, and of all I had learnt from them, I couldn't help making an exception, and saying, that there was one place where I did not like working-men at all, and that was in the public-house. 'Out of a public-house a working-man always knows how to behave to a lady; he would never think of demeaning himself by begging. I'd trust myself anywhere else to the care of working-men. But in the public-house, if a lady ventures in and gives them a few papers, or asks them to meet her on a Sunday, what is the first thing they have to say to her? "Gi'e us twopence for a pot of beer." Just like,' I added, with some asperity, 'a pig beginning to grunt for his wash the moment you approach his sty!' Up rose a hoary-headed doctor, and said, 'I think that's rather hard.' He paused. There was a suppressed stamping of feet and clapping of hands from the drinking men,—then he went on in the same dry, quiet tone,—'hard, I mean, on the *pig.*' Sudden fall of countenance in the audience. 'Did you ever see a pig go into a gin-shop at all? and did you ever see a pig take a drop too much? and, above all, did you ever see a pig go home and knock about his sow?' This last question proved irresistible; a roar of laughter greeted it, the drinking men felt they had got the worst of it, and nine of them joined the temperance club that night.

Only I would urge that free teas should not be used as a regular incentive to bring the people together to hear the gospel. This has been done in the East-end of London, and in other places, to a degree that has disgusted the more independent working-men and turned them against religion. Our Lord fed the people after they had endured fatigue and hunger to hear the gospel; He did not feed them as an inducement to get them to hear. Great as is the temptation to have constant recourse to that energetic organ, the human stomach, that never knows any religious deadness, but through all the changes and chances of this mortal life makes its voice heard the same, I cannot but believe a systematic appeal to the animal appetites must be debasing, and must act in the nature of a bribe, making the very ground rotten under one's feet.

In addition to these agencies I wish we made

more use of the children and all the fatherly love and pride which lurks in a working-man's heart, even where it seems most absent. I wish the clergy would adopt that pretty picturesque custom which still, I believe, obtains in the north, of marching all the Sunday-school children on Whit-Sunday in bright procession through the streets, all clad in their Sunday best, with banners flying, and singing hymns at the top of their glad young voices. Surely the sight of all those round and happy faces turned heavenward, the way of life strewn with fresh spring flowers, might awaken many a heart trodden down by toil and monotonous days from its sleep of indifference, and be the glad chimes to summon together a large gathering of the fathers and mothers to be held in the church after service time, or in the mission-room if spacious enough. Why should there be so little brightness and beauty in our Protestantism, so little to break through the monotonous ugliness of back streets?

In conclusion, I would earnestly point out what is one radical defect of the Church of England with regard to the working-man, what more than even her long words, long services, and pulpit English, led so many of my working-men to leave the branch of the Christian Church that had called them to Christ, and join Dissenting bodies,—a defect which, if it cannot be remedied, will always prevent the Established Church from being, what every one who loves her services must long to see her, the Church of the people. The Church of England, in one word, gives the working-man nothing to do. He feels he forms no integral part of her, that he is in no vital connection with her, that he is not built into her structure, but is left a loose stone, lying about for any one to tumble over. Methodism, on the contrary, lays hold of him, and makes him her own. He becomes a local preacher or a tract distributor, a class leader or a Sunday-school teacher, or has the care of a Band of Hope, or works in connection with a Mission-service, or the temperance cause, while he has a voice in the affairs of the chapel and in the choice of his minister. Is it any wonder, then, that, as a rule, our earnest working-men leave the church and join the chapel?

It is curious to see how this vital defect infects all the relations of the clergy with the working-man. For instance, it is a common thing in some parishes to gather together the fathers of the children who are being educated in the Church schools for a social meal, followed by a general meeting. I was present at one such meeting, where there were some four to five hundred working-men. Had it been a political meeting, any man with a grievance would have felt he had a right to stand up and speak; a good many would have joined in with some rough comments on the speeches made, possibly greatly to the speaker's embarrassment, but still with at least the admirable result of making the men feel that the political institutions of their country are their own, that they have a voice in them even when they have no vote, that the member who addresses them is emphatically *their* member. But as it was only a meeting got up by the Church—the Church in which, in theory at least, a man has a still closer ownership than in the State, the Church of which the individual stones purport to be *the man himself*—not one of those five hundred men were expected, or allowed, to take the smallest part in the meeting. Some four or five clergymen addressed them. One, being a Scotchman, exhorted them to form habits of scientific observation, and collect facts, after the example of Hugh Miller, while his hearers, being very ignorant, were probably ransacking their memories to try and recollect what part of the Bible Hugh Miller came in. But though one or two spoke admirably, not one of those five clergymen ever thought of saying to those men, 'Come now, you are the fathers of the children we are educating; you stand up and criticise our work. Let us have your opinion on it. Tell us any way you think it could be better done. How do you think your child is getting on? How do you think we could get the children to be more regular? We are trying to educate them for God; tell us where you think we fail, and how you think we could turn out better work'—so getting the men to feel that they had a voice in it all, and clergy, and fathers, and teachers were all engaged in a common work. No; there they sat, as dumb as sheep, rows and rows of patient buckets to be pumped into. One man, a good speaker, told me he did get on his legs to move a vote of thanks, but he was immediately collared by a church-warden, and cold water thrown on his laudable endeavour, as if he were a dangerous explosive.

Now, I can only say that this kind of thing will not do for working-men. If the Church of England will insist on making herself an exclusively aristocratic institution, where only broadcloth is allowed a voice and a work, she must expect to lose the democracy. Yet, surely such a Church is in a most anomalous position; recognizing a Working-man as her Lord and Head, yet tacitly excluding working-men. Surely no Christian Church would wish to find her prototype in a tailor's dog, whose master assured me he never would lie down on cloth at less than nine shillings a yard, and always flew at fustian! Must not the note of every true Christian Church be that to the poor the Gospel is preached, and among her evangelists and workers, as of old, are some who are chosen out of the people? Working-men are, by the necessities of their birth, democratic men, and as men, not as babies, must they be treated. They stoutly refuse to be strapped up in ecclesiastical perambulators and trundled along the way of salvation by either lay or clerical nurses. They hate ecclesiasticism in all its forms. But let the clergy treat them as brother men, let them give them their two great *desiderata*, work and a voice, speak to them in plain English, preach to them the human Christ, and show them hearty human fellowship, and they will find no more attached members of the Church of England than they would become.

Perhaps I shall be asked, What work? Surely there is no difficulty in finding, now-a-days, for every man his work. The Church of England Temperance movement, with the Working-men's Clubs and Bands of Hope that should belong to it, alone affords a wide field for work. On work in connexion with Mission-services I have already spoken. Where, as is frequently the case, an earnest, consistent working-man shows himself a good speaker, a working-man's mission to the neighbouring villages, with tract distribution, might be undertaken, or they might take a few back streets as their field of labour.

Do we not practically ignore the fact that our Lord chose the Apostles of the world mainly from working-men; that, probably, He had some good reason for this choice; and that, therefore, an immense, and, so far as the Established Church goes, an unused evangelistic power may be hidden away in our working-men? Surely it would be possible to organise the earnest working-men in every parish, and give them Church-work, and make them realise their Christian priesthood.

Another valuable agency, in which the help of our earnest working-men would be wanted, and which I should like to see adopted by the Church, is Adult Sunday-schools. These have been turned to admirable account by the Society of Friends. An Adult Sunday-school at Birmingham numbers a thousand men, meeting at half-past seven in the morning. One at Hitchin numbers some three hundred men, meeting at half-past two in the afternoon. Reading and writing are taught, the lower classes by working-men, the higher by educated men and women. Many a man who is too tired to learn on the week nights, thankfully embraces the opportunity presented by the long unoccupied Sunday hours, which he would otherwise have spent in the public-house. The school concludes with a short religious address and prayer. I trust I shall not have to meet any objection to writing being taught on the Sunday. As a grave mild-eyed Quaker replied to such a foolish Judaizing objector, 'Friend, does thee not think that pot-hooks are better than the pot-house on the Lord's day?' When a man has written six times down in his copy-book, with much labour of his horny palms, and much unwonted attitude of his whole person, 'Be not overcome of evil, but overcome evil with good;' or, 'No drunkard shall inherit the kingdom of heaven;' there is not much fear of his forgetting that text.

At Birmingham the movement has been taken up by the Dissenting bodies, thousands of working-men being thus under religious and secular instruction. But I am not aware of the Establised Church having adopted this valuable agency.

The real difficulty lies of course in the want of workers, our earnest capable ones being already used up for Sunday-schools and Bible-classes.

But surely many middle-class men would undertake work of this kind, who do not feel at all called to Sunday-school teaching or district-visiting; while the additional Board-schools would furnish us the buildings, hours being so arranged that the school might adjourn for the address, as at Hitchin, to some more spacious building, or perhaps to the church after afternoon service.

CHAPTER VI.

SOCIAL DIFFICULTIES.

I HAVE often been struck of late by the truth of the observation made by one of our most original but little-known thinkers,* how far our moral faculties have lagged behind our intellectual; and how little we have as yet learnt to introduce the intellectual methods into our moral life, to act on the same methods as we think.

At the very time I was conducting my moral experiment with my rough working-men, my dear father was conducting some scientific experiments for Government, on the effect of pressure on heat. But on what curiously different methods we started! To have a due regard not to some, but

* See 'Life and Letters of James Hinton. Edited by Ellice Hopkins. With an Introduction by Sir William Gull.' Second edition. C. Kegan Paul & Co.

to all the facts, to see everything not isolated, but in its relations, to bring every conclusion again to the test of facts—in one word, accuracy of regard, this is the fundamental principle of modern science. Had my father only attended to the small class of facts in which he had a personal interest as telling for him, and tending to confirm some mathematical calculations he had made, not only would his character as a scientific man have been destroyed, but such a procedure, we see at once in the intellectual life, would lead to disaster and certain wrong result. But though this is often precisely what we do in the moral life, attending only to the small class of facts that make for our own self-interest, and disregarding all others, it is not as clearly recognized that this must lead to disaster and wrong result there as well as in our intellectual life. As long as we regard a few abstract moral laws, as long as we try and love God, and pay our debts, and speak the truth, and don't take things that do not belong to us, we think we may centre our lives as much as we like about ourselves, and the facts that belong especially to us, and leave out of consideration the facts of the lives of others as that which does not concern us. We do not recognize that we must live in some sort of relation with the lives in the next back street; that our moral world, humanity itself, is as much an organic whole as the physical world of science, of which every part is dependent on every other; and in which, therefore, any element left out must produce wrong result or moral disorder. So far from recognizing this, we look upon a regard to the facts of the poorer lives around us, as a sort of superfluous goodness which it may be very nice to have, but which the majority of people may be excused for being wholly without. 'I have no taste for that kind of thing,' is the usual remark, without any of that sense of shame which a scientific man would feel in allowing that he was habitually violating the very conditions of intellectual order. Yet Christianity has but one voice, not, Save your own soul, not, Take care of your own goodness,—but, *love*, have a response to every claim upon you whether of God, of your own soul, or of others; take in *all* the facts, correlate your own life to the lives around you, be serving them directly or indirectly. How is it we put aside this voice, and so often substitute for it the traditions of men? We know that nothing will do instead of truth to fact in our intellectual life; but we think that other things —domestic virtues, punishments, poor laws, culture —will do instead of love, which is the truth to fact of the moral world.

And so it comes to pass, that side by side with that magnificent intellectual order which we call modern science, with its ever-widening achievements, there rises up the intolerable disorder of our moral and social life. The left-out elements spread confusion and wrong through the whole. The vast outcast class of lost women and children which exists at the very heart of our Christian civilizations, and whom we pure and educated Christian women carefully shutter and curtain out of our homes and very thoughts, corrupts our own sons, debases our manhood, poisons our national health, and degrades our legislation. Our selfish absorption in our own interests, caught up and echoed by the working classes, gives rise to a strife between labour and capital which perpetually threatens our trade, and engenders hatred and bitterness; while the huddled-up lives in our courts and back streets originate the germs of disease which visit impartially the rich man's house and the poor man's hovel, and indirectly give rise to drunkenness and crime, which burden us with heavy calendars and poor-rates, and darken and sadden our moral world.

And so also it was that, brought up as we all are more or less to disregard the facts of the lives of others, and have our eyes turned inward to certain great moral principles and religious truths, rather than outward to the conditions which must determine the application and working of those principles and truths, my father and I worked at our two experiments on wholly different methods. While he was not content with laying down some great well-known physical laws, and then, finding the facts not in accordance with them, laying the blame on the disorder of the physical world and the corruption of the universe, but patiently set to work to find out the disturbing causes, I found myself preaching the great truths of Christianity, and the fundamental principles of morality, very much surprised at the wrong results I came to in the lives of my hearers, but never giving a glance to the disturbing causes, or patiently searching out the unrecognized influences which were shaping those lives to evil. I am well aware that there is an arbitrary element in the moral world, in 'the unruly wills and affections of sinful men,' which there is not in the physical world; but that does not excuse us from the additional disorder and confusion we bring in by not recognizing the true method that might reduce much of the arbitrary element to the necessity which is perfect freedom, of moral law, of righteousness and holiness; by not recognizing the right aim, by not training our moral emotions by every gift of divine grace, every human endeavour, first of all to respond to every legitimate claim, and then to take in all the facts which must determine the form of the response in action; by not endeavouring to see things in their relations in the world of conduct, as well as in the world of science and intellect, and get rid of the non-regard * out of our moral

---

* I follow Mr. Hinton's example in using this rather outlandish word, as being the only word common to both the

life, as, since the rise of inductive science, we have already got rid of it out of our intellectual life.

Accordingly, in my first efforts to live in some sort of helpful relation with these rough men around me, I found myself in the position of a child who goes on perpetually doing a sum which is copied down wrong, and perpetually comes to a wrong result; while the great Master was ever saying to me, 'Look, my child, look, see if the conditions are right.' At length, by dint of much suffering over wrong results, I began to open my eyes and look at the facts of these men's lives, and to feel the absolute necessity of some social reforms before any wide-spread good could be effected. It was not much use preaching that their bodies were temples of the Holy Ghost, when the outer courts of that temple were the public-house every Saturday night. It is up-hill work inculcating thrift and saving habits on our English working-men, when they have no greater

intellectual and moral life, denoting want of truth and accuracy in the one, and selfishness in the other, selfishness being not a positive thing, but simply not looking, not regarding any facts but those that personally regard us.

inducements to save than two-and-a-half per cent., or the risks of a but too often insolvent benefit-club, with the forfeiture of parish relief as an additional stimulus to those whose aims and traditions are low. It is mockery to enforce chastity, and decent habits, and reverence for womanhood, on those who are huddled up like pigs in one room every night.

It is, therefore, on these social questions that I want to offer a few remarks and suggestions before concluding these notes on work.

First in order comes the great drinking question. My experience was the same as that of every other worker, that the public-house is the open grave of all our efforts for the good of the people.

Perhaps my friend the publican who wailed to the policeman that 'it was nothing of a trade since this here woman has been preaching,' might have comforted his heart had he known how completely the victorious enemy felt worsted by 'the trade.' I knew but too well that when the wave of religious enthusiasm had passed, the public-house was there to resume its fatal influence. And, alas! men with too often hereditary drinking habits in their blood, under the pressure of constant temptation supplied by nearly a hundred public-houses, were but too often falling back into their old vice.

I am most anxious on this difficult social problem, which at present is so completely baffling the wisest heads and strongest hearts, not to seem as if I wished to discourage any efforts that are being made, or to deny the wisdom and necessity of 'diversity of operations' animated by one spirit of love to our people, and a common desire to get rid of our national enemy. But I cannot help questioning whether we have as yet fully mastered the conditions of the problem, whether we have a due regard to all the facts, whether there are not left out elements which are reducing all our efforts at solving the problem to confusion.

One thing at least is certain. The public-house in some form or other is a necessity. Let us at least so far realise the conditions of a working-man's life as to recognize this. Working-men, I repeat, are not differently constituted from other men; however domestic a man may be, he requires the society of his fellows, he needs some place where he can see the papers, and where he can talk trade and politics. In our own rank, a man can see society in his own house, or in those of his friends, while most professional work is more or less social in its character. But the working-man cannot receive his friends in the narrow limits of his own house, and manual labour is generally accompanied by conditions unfavourable to intercourse. The public-house is the only place where he can see the more expensive public prints, keep himself *au courant* with public affairs, where he can transact the business of clubs, etc., where he can hear of jobs of work. The club-house, though not ranking above a convenient luxury in our class, is an absolute necessity to working-men.

But can the public-house as at present constituted ever be reformed, even by that potent moraliser of the British mind—an Act of Parliament? Even if, in the face of the enormous vested interests, we could get a really effective legislation, is it not radically vicious, a decayed tooth in the social organization, only capable of the drastic remedy of extraction?

Not only is a man forced to take alcoholic

drinks for the good of the house,—tea, coffee, and other unintoxicating beverages not being provided; not only are all its traditions and its public opinion on the side of drunkenness, so that no one feels disgraced if a man exceeds, but its tenure is too often hopelessly bad. The majority of public-houses are owned by brewers, which in itself secures the drink traffic being doubly and artificially stimulated. Some of the largest public-houses in the place where I worked, were on what is called 'barrel rent,' that is, the publican had the house rent-free on condition of his consuming a certain number of barrels of beer. In Liverpool the public-houses are getting more and more into the hands of a few wealthy brewers, whose profits are so enormous, that even if they and not their managers were made responsible, they would still be beyond the reach of a system of legislative fines, and can afford to snap their fingers at the law. At present they are practically irresponsible; they offer up their managers as a scape-goat to the claims of the law, and put in another who does the same thing, only with a little more caution.

If flying from this evil we take refuge in the

Gothenburg system, and advocate the public-houses being bought up and vested in the town council,—to say nothing of the enormous outlay to begin with, it places what one cannot but feel to be a dangerous power in the hands of that body, involving for its right exercise an incorruptibility, a disinterested public spirit, and a practical wisdom which have not proved universally characteristic of corporations, with that want of individual responsibility which Sydney Smith characterized in his caustic remark, that 'they had neither a body to be kicked nor a soul to be damned.'

Turn which way you will—that is to say if the vested interests permitted us to turn at all, which at present they do not—one gets gored by one or the other horn of a dilemma: make your licensing system strict, and you throw the trade into the hands of a few wealthy monopolists, who have capital enough to render their sumptuous gin-palaces irresistibly attractive, power enough to defy or evade the law. On the other hand make your licensing system loose, give up restrictive measures, and go in for free trade, and you have the multiplication of public-houses, which wrung the cry from the poor wife endeavouring to shepherd her husband home from his work, 'I *could* get him past two, but, oh, sir, I can't get him past ten!'

To the permissive bill I do not allude. If the story of the Kilkenny cats be, indeed, the great epic of humanity under a figure, then let us go in for it—the two tails I presume representing two empty beer-pots, which will survive the destruction of our race. If an internecine conflict renewed every year, with the hatred, the party spirit, the corruption that belongs to internecine conflicts, will add to the beauty and dignity of human life; if a remedy so drastic that its only cure is amputation, without the power of palliation if amputation is impossible, is the last and most enlightened outcome of moral therapeutics; if a system so partial in its operation that, in closing the public-houses of one district, it must necessarily glut the public-houses of the next, commends itself as likely to conduce to public order, or minister to the good of the part unenlightened as well as part enlightened whole—let us have it. If there is no alternative it may possibly be our duty to go in for it, as better on the whole than the present state of things; but it certainly will not be with a 'light heart' on the part of those who reflect, or who are endowed with less irrepressible spirits than Sir Wilfrid Lawson.*

I would, therefore, urge that the public-house is vicious in principle, that it contains no moral element, which, in dealing with so powerful an agent as intoxicants, is an absolutely necessary factor, and one which cannot be supplied by

---

* Since writing the above Sir Wilfrid Lawson and his supporters have offered to unite in supporting some more moderate and workable measure, in the hope that it may prove a step towards ultimately passing their Permissive Bill; so we may now hope that some common platform may be devised which will unite our scattered forces against the common enemy. Surely the success of the school-board in dealing with the vast question of elementary education points to some sort of licensing-board elected by the ratepayers, and not involved, like the Town Council, in a multitude of other interests and the mazes of local politics, but brought into existence solely for grappling with the difficulties that beset the regulation of the liquor traffic. Why should not some wealthy public-spirited town like Birmingham, which can re-create a public library in a few days, be empowered by Parliament to try the experiment, and work out useful results for the rest of England?

legislative enactments from without. Practically it seems to be constantly overlooked that the old tavern bore precisely the same fruits in our own class as it is now bearing in the lower classes: that fifty or sixty years ago our class was as given to drinking habits as the working-classes are now; and not till the club took the place of the tavern did a better state of public opinion arise, and a consequent diminution of drunkenness.

I cannot, therefore, but feel that the energy of the country has gone too much into a direct attack upon 'the drink,' without sufficiently considering its causes, leading to a considerable waste of energy in the endeavour to make all men total abstainers, which seems to me a wholly visionary enterprise; and giving rise to that curious modern Manichæism which places the sin in the drink itself, in what Milton calls the 'matter of the sin,' leading even educated men to commit themselves in public to such an absurdly identical proposition as 'the cause of drunkenness is the drink,' which conveys about as much valuable information as if I were to say the cause of shoes is the shoemaker.

Let me not be misunderstood. I believe our debt to total abstinence is immense. It has led to a searching investigation of the uses of alcohol that would not have taken place under the pressure of a less extreme system, and which has already introduced the most extensive modifications into medical practice and private habits, and will probably work a good deal further in this direction. It has convinced us of the utter absurdity of our drinking customs, of the daily excess we are often guilty of in amount even when considering ourselves patterns of sobriety, and of the extreme danger of having recourse to alcohol on ordinary occasions of nervous exhaustion and fatigue, instead of adopting Sir William Gull's simple plan of taking a few raisins when too tired for ordinary food. But however great a work total abstinence is doing in hygiene, always so closely allied to our moral life, and with whatever loving reverence I look on the personal sacrifice, in countless cases not for themselves but for others, which has given rise to so large a body of total abstainers, as a cure for the great moral evil of drunkenness, it has the same inherent weakness as all restrictive systems, and while conferring much partial benefit, will fail in its wider aim, as celibacy in the middle ages failed as a cure for the evils of licentiousness. Intemperance now increases in the teeth of all its efforts, admirable as these efforts have been. It will always remain, I believe, a useful factor in that exceedingly complex thing, human life, necessary for some, and often a help, even though rather an ascetic help, towards realising that 'plain living and high thinking,' in which modern life, in its rebound from asceticism, is so grievously wanting. As a protest against the present excess, and as an expression of fellowship and sympathy with those who are trying to overcome their drinking habits, thoughtful people might do well to adopt it, if they are able ; but exalted into a system, and looked upon not as *a* cure, but as the only cure of intemperance, I fear it is doomed to disappointment. It is for this reason I regret so much of the energy of the country having gone so exclusively into this channel, and a direct attack upon 'the drink,' instead of on the causes of the drink.

To take an instructive simile from Herbert

Spencer:—'You see that this wrought iron plate is not flat; it sticks up a little towards the left, "cockles," as we say. How shall we flatten it? Obviously, you reply, by hitting down on the part that is prominent. Well, here is a hammer, and I give the plate a blow as you advise. Harder, you say. Still no effect. Another stroke. Well, there is one, and another, and another. The prominence remains, you see: the evil is as great as ever, greater, indeed. But this is not all. Look at the warp which the plate has got near the opposite edge. Where it was flat before it is now curved. A pretty bungle we have made of it. Instead of curing the original defect we have produced a second. Had we asked an artizan practised in "planishing," as it is called, he would have told us that no good was to be done, but only mischief, by hitting down on the projecting part. He would have taught us how to give variously directed and specially adjusted blows with a hammer elsewhere, so attacking the evil not by direct, but indirect actions. The required process is less simple than you thought. Even a sheet of metal is not to be successfully dealt with after those common-sense methods in which you have so much confidence.' *

Now, have we not, in Herbert Spencer's words, hit down too directly at drunkenness, aiming directly at the results, instead of indirectly at the causes, so that, as in the iron plate, the evil has grown and is growing in the very face of all our efforts? Should we not meet with more success if we were steadily to recognize these three points: first, that the public-house of entertainment is a necessity in the working-man's life, and cannot be suppressed; secondly, that the public-house, the tavern, as presenting no moral element, except an evil one, is radically defective, and subject to abuses; thirdly, that the club, with its absence of vicious self-interest enlisted in the drink traffic, with its *esprit de corps*, and its character to sustain, does present, both positively and negatively, the necessary moral influences to control the use of intoxicants, or to dispense with them altogether, as may be thought best; and if, while still endeavouring to procure an amendment of our licensing laws, we were to throw our chief energies into

* Herbert Spencer's Study of Sociology, chap. xi., 271.

getting the club substituted for the public-house?

With regard to the basis on which these clubs are established, whether on total abstinence principles or not, I can only state that so far as intemperance is concerned it is not a vital question. The majority of the working-men's clubs, now amounting to upwards of eight hundred, are not teetotal; but there is no drunkenness among their members. Even when spirits as well as beer are admitted this is the case; the consumption in one London club, for many hundreds of men, only amounting to two or three bottles a week. The large club-house which was raised by my dear father's exertions in connection with my work, was at first opened on total abstinence principles, but beer has been since admitted with no evil results. Indeed, Mr. Hodgson Pratt, the Chairman of the Working-Men's Club and Institute Union, states that their almost invariable experience is that the quantity of intoxicants consumed steadily diminishes after the first opening of a club. In one large club in the North they doubled their members and halved their consumption of beer by the end of the first year. On a rough north-country fellow being asked the reason of this anomalous result, 'Well, sir, I dunno' how it is; but ye see we've so mooch a gooin' on with lectures, and singin', and readin's, and entertainments, that somehoo we've no time to think aboot the beer.' The beer was in fact, as our American friends say, fairly 'crowded out.' In another very large club lately formed in the East End of London among the lowest costermongers, the members are possessed with a raging desire to improve their minds, while at the same time they greatly object to being preached at. Amongst other distinguished men, they sent a deputation to Cardinal Manning to request him to come and address them on Sunday, but added that they made only two stipulations with His Eminence, that he must not talk to them about religion, and he must not talk to them about temperance! Like a wise man, he at once cordially accepted their invitation, and was listened to by a most attentive and appreciative audience, the men sitting with their pots of beer before them in case His Eminence proved a thought dry, their wives sitting peacefully by their sides with the last baby at their breast; and I have no doubt no one would have suspected from the nature of the discourse the severe surgical operation the eloquent cardinal had submitted to at their hands, of having both his legs cut off.

Of course, where the rough and costermonger element is large, some time must be allowed for their gradually working up to the standard of sobriety and choice language we should like; but at the same time, let us be thankful that the drunkenness that fills the mouth with oaths and obscenity, and vents itself in kicks to the wife and blows to the child, is got rid of. The mere fact that they get pure undrugged beer goes a long way in itself to secure this result. At first they don't quite know what to make of it, but they soon grow very much to prefer it. And the sense of *esprit dé corps*, of the character of the club to keep up, and the growing feeling that drunkenness is disgraceful and wasteful, does the rest. Indeed the sooner we disabuse ourselves of the idea that a working-man cannot control himself unless he be bandaged up with pledges and restrictions the better. Once rid them of a vicious public-house system, it will be found that their clubs are, as a rule, as sober and well-conducted as ours.

'But why not advocate the establishment of coffee-palaces, which are open to all, and where any one could go and get good coffee when he pleases, just as freely as he can go to a public-house?' perhaps some one will ask; 'why restrict it to the members of a club? why not throw the building open to the public?'

Do you quite understand the problem you have got to solve? I answer to those who talk thus. Doubtless coffee-palaces are admirable things, and I not only advocate them, but advocate their being multiplied tenfold in every large town. They will do much to educate all classes alike out of our present ridiculous dependence on alcoholic drinks, as if they were the necessary concomitant of every social and kindly feeling. But however important is the function coffee-palaces may fulfil, they will not prove a substitute for the public-house, in other words, they may take the outworks of intemperance, but they will leave its citadel untouched. As a rule working-men do not use them as an evening resort, for the simple reason that they do not afford quiet separate rooms where they can feel at home, and where they can smoke their pipes and do as they like. And I would earnestly point out it is the evening resort that must ever be the stronghold of drunkenness. Men don't go to the public-house on purpose to get drunk. In all my wide experience I have only known one case of a man who went with the deliberate intention of getting drunk, who sat down all by himself and went steadily at it. It is the company and good fellowship that lead to it, and what we want is something that takes hold of this company and good fellowship feeling, and makes it a force on the side of decent behaviour, as the public-house takes hold of it and makes it a force on the side of indecent behaviour; that makes it a principle of orderly conduct, instead of a principle of disorderly rows; and this the club element, and that element alone, does, with suitable premises necessary to its develop-

SOCIAL DIFFICULTIES.

ment, and of which the club must have the exclusive ownership.

But even in those rare cases where the upper premises of a coffee-palace are let off for the exclusive use of a working-man's club, there is the great disadvantage of the club being forced to adopt total abstinence principles, whether they wish it or not, since intoxicants are not allowed on the premises. In the case of voluntary teetotalers, this would lead to no evil; but with those who are not, it leads to their going to the public-house to get the glass of beer which they cannot procure at their club. And I would again urge that you will never attack drunkenness in the mass on principles of total abstinence. Admirable and successful as its efforts are with the individual, the mass will never come under its influence. Why, the mass of the clergy and ministers of religion, certainly taking their small pay and hard work, the most self-denying class of men we have, are not total abstainers. Why do we expect of working-men a self-denial which in the mass we do not practise ourselves? Are God's ten commandments so very easy to keep that we must be perpetually adding an eleventh of our own? Let us master the ten first before we go on to an eleventh, which makes it a sin for a working-man, not for ourselves, to take a glass of small beer in his club.

But, at the risk of wearisome repetition, I must again say, that when you admit intoxicants you must also secure a moral element, the social *esprit de corps* of a well-organized club, to control them. The admission of beer into coffee-palaces and British-Workmen, would, I fear, in the end, generate the old abuses of the public-house over again.

I trust, however, because I advocate the club principle as a good one, I shall not be accused of the folly of looking upon clubs as a complete panacea. Clubs are no ideal institutions, they are liable to abuse like everything else. One may drink condemnation out of the chalice itself, if one be so minded. Many working-men's clubs are, I have no doubt, low and secularist in tone, and a few may be accompanied with grave abuses, though these latter are the exception. But I contend that the want of a higher tone is in great part owing to the life of the Christian Church, and the efforts of educated men having flowed almost exclusively into other channels. Had there been earnest co-operation, on the part of the clergy especially, with the working-men in their movement for securing some respectable substitute for the public-house, had there been that hearty mingling of educated and uneducated on Club Committees, the tone of the existing clubs would unquestionably be higher, and working-men would not have once more discovered that modern Christianity is out of sympathy with them and their difficulties, that it has no keen understanding of them and their wants, and how best to meet them, and would not have learned a fresh lesson in their favourite thesis, that they 'don't see the good of religion.'

I would, therefore, have every clergyman feel that the parish is simply disgraced that offers no substitute for the public-house; that he has no right to preach the gospel while leaving his people hopelessly exposed to a sure and deadly evil, any more than he would have to preach the laws of health over an open drain. Meetings of working-men should be at once held, some well-known and popular speaker should be secured, bills being distributed at all the public-houses, and left at each door; some local doctor should display gorgeously-coloured diagrams of the results of drinking to the internal organs, the inflammation being emphasized by much expenditure of vermilion; statistical statements should be made, both general and local, of the amount of money spent in drink, and what the money might effect if spent on their own homes, and an earnest appeal made to the better man in them, while an offer of help should be made to meet the expenses of starting a club of their own in some temporary room or existing public-house, if such can be found.* It is a curious fact, and one that is a source of some anxiety to those who are interested in the club movement, and see in it one of the most

* Any one wishing to start a Working-Men's Club has only to apply to the Secretary of the Working-Men's Club and Institute Union, 150, Strand, and he will be at once supplied with every possible information of the most valuable and practical kind.

hopeful and practical ways of getting rid of intemperance, that owing to the want of public interest and co-operation, wealthy brewers are beginning to offer to advance the funds for establishing the proper premises for a working-man's club, on condition, of course, of securing the custom of the club in addition to a fair rate of interest on their money. I do not myself think this a fatal arrangement by any means, the brewer having no tool like the publican to exalt his interests at the price of the public good; and as brewers are born with consciences like other men, there are many who would doubtless very much prefer to carry on a profitable business without the sense of bringing wide-spread misery and ruin into so many homes, which must occasionally visit the owners of public-houses. But I think we must be all agreed that it is most undesirable that the club should have any direct connexion with the drinking trade; and it is for public-spirited men and women to prevent this, by coming forward and offering the capital needed for securing suitable premises.

With regard to the basis adopted, whether total abstinence or moderation, it should be left to the members of the club when formed to decide, all attempts at meddling and dictation being simply fatal with anything to do with working-men. Brotherly help from a man or a woman of superior station to their own they are in general most grateful for; and their defect of jealousy and distrust of one another, which belongs to all uneducated people, makes such co-operation peculiarly valuable to them; but freedom to manage their own affairs in their way, not perhaps ours, they will and must have.

To those who fear the encroachment of the club on the homes, I would suggest it is useless fearing what already exists; the worst, the most hopeless encroachment on the home is the public-house. I used to tell the public-house men that they were unworthy of the grand old English name of husbands; they were house-breakers, not house-bands, squandering on the publican and his wife the time and money wanted at home. But I believe all custodians of clubs would pretty much echo the experience of one who told me that at first he was much discouraged by observing that his new members after a time ceased to come every evening, and only turned up once or twice in the week. But on asking the reason, he was told, 'Well, don't ye see when I went to the public I used never to think of stopping at home, but now that we have got things a bit comfortable-like, why I likes to sit with my old missus sometimes when I comes in tired.'

Clubs for big lads up to the age when they can safely be admitted among the men, are of the utmost importance, but if established under the same roof, they must have a separate room and separate entrances. Any attempt to mix them is always fatal.

A club-house might also be so arranged as to have a public bar where coffee and other non-intoxicants and light refreshments might be supplied to the general public, without interfering with the comfort and privacy of the club.

But no one specific will ever cure our great national evil. In our moral 'planishing,' our blows must be variously directed. Merely to sweep and to do up the house, if it be left empty, is not enough to expel the evil spirit. Doubtless one of the great causes of drunkenness is the dulness, the monotony of life, the daily grind which presses heavily on us all at times, but especially on those engaged in manual labour, particularly among the more shut-up people of the north, that pathetic longing that poor human nature has to be a little jolly under the adverse conditions the world affords, to dance even though it be on a rotten plank. Education will doubtless be a great help to us here, in placing a wider range and a better class of amusements within the reach of the people. But let us not put a superstitious trust in its efficacy. Let us not forget that education is nothing in itself, only an added capacity for good or for evil. If we look not wisely on the sun himself, he smites us into darkness, says Milton; and the good of education, like light, depends on what use we put it to. Scotland is better educated than the English people can hope to be in two generations, yet Scotland is more drunken than England. And may not the Puritanic feeling against amusements, which is more rife in Scotland even than in England, be much to blame here? If Wesley could not see why the devil should have all the good tunes, still les should we be able to see why he should have all the good amusements. That some have been put to a bad use is no reason for rejection. It is no use quarrelling with hemp because some men hang themselves with it. We need to claim every amusement which can be carried on without betting, gambling, and drinking, and yield a little pleasurable excitement which does not end like the excitement of the drink, in what has been called the 'foot and mouth disease,' the excitement that goes in at the mouth and comes out at the heavy boots, in kicking wife or child. Billiards, bagatelle, skittles, cricket, croquet, chess, draughts, dominoes,—nay, I believe my soul is stout enough to contemplate even beggar-my-neighbour without quailing, provided there be no gambling,—anything that may innocently fill the empty place of the beer pot; let us claim and make good use of them all.

A good deal more might be done with music, especially in the direction of brass bands. The expense of the instruments is a difficulty, of course, but this might be paid partly in instalments, partly by subscriptions.

And might we not make some use of one of the most powerful recreations of the human mind in all ages—acting, from dumb crambo and charades up to simple little plays, illustrative of temperance, or happy home life. I shall be told at once that this would be most dangerous, as giving a taste for the theatre; but in the same way music may give a taste for the low music-halls. Would it not be wiser to recognize that these tastes do exist with or without us, and that if we won't give them wholesome food, they will get unwholesome? 'Empty by filling' is the motto of Christianity. Place the worst pig-wash under the well-head, and it disappears of itself. And surely that which afforded the noblest education to the people in ancient times that the world has ever seen; and that which in a more private form has found its way into our Bible, in the exquisite little love-drama of the Shulamite and her shepherd lover,— unquestionably a dramatic performance, and probably acted at wedding-feasts and private entertainments,—cannot be hopelessly bad, nor deserve the indiscriminate stigma the religious world has fastened upon it.

SOCIAL DIFFICULTIES.

Few things, I think, fill one with a deeper melancholy than the contemplation of the amusements of our English people, as they at present exist, or the apathy and the impenetrable narrowness of the religious world with regard to this vital question. If we denied to ourselves what we deny to the people, the spectacle we present on this point would be more bearable. But though our educated lives are far less monotonous in their wider interests than the uneducated, we are careful enough to secure our own share of amusement, and pleasant occasional breaks to the monotony of life. We have our tours abroad, our pleasant seaside change, our agreeable visits at a friend's house, shooting, fishing, music, lectures, entertainments of all kinds. But Professor Stanley Jevons, in his admirable article on the 'Amusements of the People,'* scarcely exaggerates when he remarks, 'It is hardly too much to say that the right to dwell in a grimy street, to drink freely in the neighbouring public-houses, and to walk freely between the high-walled parks, and the jealously preserved estates of our landowners,

* See *Contemporary Review*, October 1878.

is all that the just and equal laws of England secure to the mass of the population.'

The consequence of this selfish indifference of the higher and educated classes has been in England a steady degradation of the amusements of the people, which perhaps reaches its culminating point in the ordinary music hall, desecrating the very name of music, it being impossible for language to describe, as Professor Jevons observes, 'the mixture of inane songs, of senseless burlesques, and of sensational acrobatic tricks, which make the staple of a music-hall entertainment, to say nothing of the far graver moral drawbacks.'

Why should these things be? Is our English nation, which gave birth to Shakespeare and Milton, more degraded by nature than any other? Why should our noble people present on this one point such a humiliating contrast to other nations? I remember a German doctor telling me that when he was a boy at school, he and his schoolfellows went for a walking tour in the Tyrol, and on one occasion they had all to litter down on the floor of a little village inn, where they were kept awake till twelve o'clock by the blacksmith, the shoemaker, the baker, and one or two other village functionaries, performing admirably string quartets, and quintets from Beethoven, Mozart, and Haydn! Or take the American lady, whose butcher lingers on the threshold after delivering the last joint at her door, to discuss the merits of Tennyson's last poem. Or by way of contrast on a still wider scale, take Professor Jevons's description of the Tivoli gardens at Copenhagen, with a large partially open music pavilion, and a fine string orchestra, and semi-classical concerts every evening throughout the summer, attended by the Royal Family, and all classes down to artizans, and decent working folk, the seats being purposely priced very low. Why should not this kind of thing be possible in England, gradually educating our people's tastes to better and higher things? The climate of Denmark is not better than our own, nor are the people more musical. Why should not the London parks, and the public grounds of our large towns, have each their music pavilion, and their outdoor concerts in the summer evenings, well supplied with light unintoxicating beverages? Why should not Professor Jevons's suggestion be acted on, of turning the Columbia Hall into a place of recreation for the people, with a good supply of swings, merry-go-rounds, and the like? Why should lawn-tennis, croquet, golf, and other harmless games, be the exclusive property of the rich, so that the outdoor amusements of the people are reduced to squirting at one another with detestable metal pipes, and playing at kiss-in-the-ring? We have taken a few first steps in the right direction. The Crystal Palace, of which the Manager boasts with just pride that not one person in a million among visitors is charged with drunken and disorderly conduct, the Brighton and Westminster Aquariums, have proved that our people are just as capable of good and undebased amusements as any other; all we now want is that the necessity for it should be recognised, and the means for procuring it, under the higher forms and good moral regulations which will secure the union of all classes, should be provided in all our towns and villages.

There is an obvious practical measure which

at least we might embark in without seriously irritating that sensitive but much-enduring organ, the pocket of ratepayers, and that is, providing the suburbs of London with seats. At present there are millions and millions of people traversing hundreds of miles of streets without a chance of sitting down, except in or just outside a public-house, where they must drink to pay for the rest, and poison their stomachs to relieve their legs.

'Only think,' says an East End worker, 'that to these millions the streets are their recreation ground, their drawing-room, the only place where they meet their sweethearts, or talk with their friends; the place they call home is too often only a corner to sleep and eat in; all the rest of their life is passed in the work-shop or the street. Yet we won't let them sit down! Surely there is no sin in sitting out of doors. Look at an unoccupied house or shop anywhere in East London, and see how its doorsteps are crowded. Many respectable householders throw a pail of water on their steps to prevent their being sat upon. Yet our public thoroughfares, notably Bow Road, are broad enough to admit seats without the least inconvenience, and seem planted with trees on purpose; and there are waste corners, often under the dead wall that bounds a work-shop, where very sheltered seats might stand, annoying nobody. In fact, I fancy these seats would rather tend to public order, and prevent groups of people standing against houses to conduct business or arguments, often a cause of much annoyance.'

Of the higher influences, of that which pre-eminently empties by filling, filling with higher instincts, higher aims, higher hopes, till there is no place found for the low and the animal, I have already spoken. Where there is a great indifference to religion, a debating or Mutual Improvement Society, in which one of the subjects for discussion should be religion, the working-men giving their own views on it, is one of the best agencies for awakening an interest, and may lead on to a Bible-class. It is no use thrusting the Bible down their throats; but they should be led to look upon it, *as it is*, as eminently the working-men's book, chiefly the inspired sayings and doings of working-men; from David the shepherd, and Amos the herdsman, Peter and

John the fishermen, up to One chosen out of the people, of Whom it was said in contempt, Is not this the carpenter? A simple service held in their own club-room on Sundays, if the members do not object, is often better than any Mission-room.

CHAPTER VII.

THE SAVINGS QUESTION.

CLOSELY allied with the great drinking question, comes the question of the people's savings. 'Good husbandry,' says De Foe, 'is no English virtue. It may have been brought over, and in some places where it has been planted, it has thriven well enough; but it is a foreign species; it neither loves, nor is beloved by, Englishmen.' From De Foe downwards, we have been apt to contemplate our national spendthrift habits with a sort of wasteful fatalism, as though there were an inherent tendency in English nature to squander. Some of our leading men have even maintained that thrift cannot be expected to form an attribute of a bold and progressive type of national character like our own. But modern science *is* teaching us to look with suspicion on all specific tendencies, as only another name for our own ignorance and want of patient observation. Here, again, instead of indulging in abstract considerations of national character, would it not be better patiently to regard the facts?

The first fact that strikes one is unquestionably a very grave one: that so few of the working-men, so far fewer in proportion than in other countries, are possessed of capital. England, the wealthiest country in the world, also has the largest *proletariat*. Two-thirds of the population, it has been computed, are dependent on wages, and the mass of them live literally from hand to mouth.

The fact is soon stated; but perhaps it is impossible to estimate the evils and dangers that lie hidden in it. Not only does it keep the mass of the wage-receiving class for ever living on the verge of disaster, liable by the inherent fluctuations of trade to be reduced to want of the necessaries of life, and to dependence on public or private aid; not only does it place the working-classes in that disastrous antagonism with the capital in which they have no share which threatens the prosperity of our trade, but it forms an element of instability both in the national history and in individual character which it is difficult to estimate.

A great contractor for foreign railways, on being asked by Professor Fawcett which he preferred employing, English or Italian navvies, replied that, on the whole, he preferred Italian navvies; for though the English navvy could do double and even treble the day's work, he lost so much time, and gave so much trouble in drinking and fighting, that as a rule the sober, industrious Italian answered the best. On being asked why there should be this difference of conduct, he answered at once, 'Oh, the Italian is saving up his money to buy a little bit of land,—the one ambition of his heart,—and he has none to waste. The Englishman has nothing to look forward to, he has no particular inducement to save, and everything goes in drink.'

In a rich manufacturing country like England, where the land is of limited extent, and great

THE SAVINGS QUESTION. 141

wealth accumulates in the hands of a few capitalists, land, as conferring some social distinction, must gain an artificial value, which, do away with the law of primogeniture and all legal tying-up and complexities to-morrow, would still interfere with peasant proprietorship in England, and have a tendency to mass the land in the hands of a few wealthy proprietors. Nor, indeed, with the more lucrative avenues of trade open to him, would our English working-man be content to exercise the extreme frugality, thrift, and hard living involved in peasant proprietorship. The Italian labourer's inducement to save is therefore not to be had for the Englishman. But land is not the only investment. Why should there not be a proportionate number in England of peasant proprietors of capital? Why have the labouring classes no share in the capital which has been called 'crystallized labour'? It was not always so; both the yeoman and the weaver were possessed of capital in the form of a small holding, or a hand-loom; but with the merging of small holdings into large properties, and of handlooms into larger mills, there has been a steady deterioration in this respect. As Mr. Frederic Seebohm observes in an able article in the *Edinburgh Review*,* 'With the loss of the hereditary nest-egg of capital, has come the loss of the hereditary habit of thrift and saving.'

But has not the same want of seeing, which I complain of in the moral life, the same want of one-tenth of the careful observation and taking in of all the facts of the moral problem which would be bestowed as a matter of course on a problem in chemistry, been largely at fault here as elsewhere? Not only is our poor law a gigantic discouragement of saving, a systematic recognition that the able-bodied labourer, subject to no particular disaster, for which exceptional provision could be made, cannot save, but must be provided for by the State in his old age or sickness, though it is a statistical fact that the working-classes spend £30,000,000 per annum in drink and tobacco; but the efforts of the State to work in an opposite direction have been singularly unfortunate. The whole

---

* The Savings of the People: *Edinburgh Review*, July 1873.

influence of both Government and individuals, till lately, has gone into encouraging benefit clubs, the one form of saving which accumulates no capital, and which is most exposed to miscalculation and fraud. The very endeavour on the part of the State to save the funds from the latter, by offering Government security with the additional bait of 4½ per cent., proved most injurious in the end, as the gradual reduction of the interest in itself produced the danger of insolvency to the clubs, while the Exchequer suffered a loss of not much less than £1,000,000. Indeed, so precarious is this form of investment both from the extreme complexity of the calculation in compound interest it requires to regulate the rate of payment, and also from the liability to fraud, that it is calculated that some 70 per cent. of the benefit clubs are insolvent. Unquestionably the breaking-up of so many has given a most grievous check to saving on the part of the people.

But already matters have taken a more hopeful turn, and the conditions are being realized for the creation of capital in the hands of the working-classes.

First in order and importance comes the Post Office Savings Bank, which has formed the most valuable elementary school in thrift of modern times.

'As early as the year 1807,' a writer in the *British Quarterly** narrates, 'Mr. Whitbread in the House of Commons foreshadowed the present Post Office Savings Bank scheme, in a remarkable speech on the Poor Laws Amendment Bill. He recommended the institution of a Government Savings Bank, to be worked with the Post Office machinery, the money received to be invested in Government stock, the annual limit of deposits to be £20 and the total limit £200. But Mr. Whitbread lived in advance of his time; the idea was feebly praised by the few, pooh-poohed by an overwhelming majority, and was at last abandoned. In course of time, however, it was revived, and put to more definite uses by one of the most notable of all the labourers in this field of philanthropy, Mr. Sikes of Huddersfield. Mr. Whitbread had laboured, Mr. Sikes entered into his labours, and carried them forward with such pertinacity and unflagging zeal that he

* On Savings Banks: *British Quarterly*, January 1878.

THE SAVINGS QUESTION. 145

forced his views into prominence, and demonstrated so clearly the possibility of establishing successful Government Savings Banks through the intervention of the Money-order department of the Post Office, that there was no resisting him or his arguments. But Mr. Sikes could not master the whole details of the scheme, and it was reserved for Mr. Chetwynd, at that time a staff officer in the Money-order department of the General Post Office, to bring his thorough practical knowledge to shape the theories of the philanthropist into a compact and workable form. Even then it needed wheel within wheel to put the machinery in motion; and the finishing strokes and minor details were supplied by Mr. Scudamore, the receiver and accountant-general of the Post Office. In building and launching this new ship of State, it may be said that Mr. Whitbread collected the raw material,—the wood and iron, the planks and the masts; Mr. Sikes put them into shape, and reared the ship upon the stocks; Mr. Chetwynd supplied the ropes and sails, the rudder and compass; and Mr. Scudamore marked out the vessel's course and noted in the chart all rocks and reefs and dangerous tides and eddies.'

On September 16th, 1862, the ship thus built was launched, and, in the language of a contemporary *Times*, 'the country soon recognized the universal boon of a bank maintained at the public expense, secured by the public responsibility, with the whole empire for its capital, with a branch in every town, open at almost all hours, and, more than all, giving a fair amount of interest.'

On referring to the last report of the Postmaster-General, issued in September 1878, we see at once the extraordinary progress that has been made in educating the people to save by this one agency alone. During the sixteen years that Post Office Savings Banks have been in existence, the total sum standing to their credit on the books of the National Debt Commissioners at the close of the year, was in 1862 £1,659,032, and in 1877 £29,713,529, while the number of depositors in the old Savings Banks and Post Office Savings Banks combined, has risen from 1,732,555 to 3,301,087.

THE SAVINGS QUESTION.

In 1877 the proportion of depositors to population was one to nineteen in the United Kingdom, or one to fifteen in England and Wales, one to seventy-four in Scotland, and one to eighty-two in Ireland.

A far greater number of deposits are made in December and January than in any other time of the year. The largest amount received in any one day during the year 1877 was on the 31st of December, when the total was 25,857, amounting to £83,590 6s. 3d. The average daily number of deposits is 10,659.

These statistics will give our readers some idea of the enormous mass of business that is carried on in connection with our Post Office Savings Banks. To conduct it there are no less than 493 officers and clerks, of whom ninety are women, in the Central Savings Banks Department, London, exclusive of clerks for extra duty, writers, sorters, messengers, porters, etc.; and the total expenses for working the whole of the vast machinery of the Post Office Savings Bank is given in the revenue estimates for the year ending March 31st, 1878, as £134,057.

It is a striking instance of the hour-hand-like slowness with which the British mind moves, that so obvious an anomaly as the difference of interest between the old trustee Savings Banks and the new Post Office Savings Banks has never been removed. As long ago as 1866, Mr. Lewin writes in his admirable 'History of Savings Banks:' 'The old Savings Banks deposit their funds with Government, and are allowed interest on their money at the rate of £3 5s. per cent. The Post Office Banks of course deposit their money with Government, and are allowed interest at the rate of £2 10s. per cent. Out of the 15s. per cent. difference between the two rates, an average of half of it is given by the old banks to their depositors.

'Now it is well known that the average cost of each transaction in the Post Office Banks is little more than half the average cost of a transaction in the ordinary Savings Banks.* If

* The writer in the *British Quarterly* states that the average cost of a transaction in the Post Office Saving's Banks during the whole period of their existence has been $6\frac{1}{10}d.$, as compared with 1s. in the old Savings Banks.

Government can still afford to pay the old Savings Banks the higher rate of interest, it might afford at the least computation to give 10*s.* per cent. more to depositors in the Post Office Savings Banks. If Government cannot afford to pay the higher rate, it ought to discontinue its charity, which, like all other charitable doles, excites discontent among those who think they have, and really have the right *de facto*, if not *de jure*, to share it. That the rate should be equalized in one way or the other admits, we think, of little question; but that the Government should pay more than it can pay without loss, admits of less.'

Equalize the rate of interest, and the old trustee Savings Banks, with their liability to fraud, and their greater expense of management, would be quickly absorbed into the more economical and safer system of the Post Office Savings Banks. It has been calculated that the Government might effect an ultimate saving of £280,000 by closing the old Savings Banks altogether. I question whether any other civilized Government but England's would calmly display for upwards of sixteen years such an anomaly as a bounty offered to the poor out of the public funds to induce them to invest their savings in a less perfect security, when it offers them a perfect security at the hands of its own officials and at no loss to itself!

Another reform which is urgently needed, and which would add greatly to the value of the Post Office Bank, is the extension of the narrow limit of the annual deposit. At present the depositor is limited to £30 per annum, and to £150 in all. On this point bankers have persistently opposed their selfish interest to the public good; but the example of other countries shows how little justice there is in the opposition they have maintained in England. In France the limit is £40; in Belgium, £120; in Denmark there is no limit; in some parts of Prussia, £150; in Switzerland, it varies from a very small sum to £400; and in Austria, from £50 to £1,500. If the statutory limit in England were even raised to £50, it would be a great gain, that being a convenient sum to invest.

The Post Office Savings Bank is doing good service in affiliating Penny Banks. In 1877 no less than 293 Penny Banks received authority to invest their funds in the Post Office Savings Bank, showing an increase of 121 over the previous year. The establishment of Penny Banks, in connection especially with Board Schools, following the precedent of a successful movement first set on foot in Belgium, 'is destined,' writes the Postmaster-General, 'to play a very important part in developing thrift and saving habits, judging by the results already attained.' As an example of the success of these banks, the forty penny banks in operation in the London Board Schools received in the year ending 31st December, 1877, in deposits, £3,007, from 9,611 children. The remarkable increase in the total amount of deposits in French savings banks within the last three years, from £20,600,000 to £32,360,000, though partly attributable to the material prosperity of France, is supposed to be mainly due to the extraordinary development in the three last years of penny and school savings banks brought about by the efforts of M. Auguste de Malarce.

As Working-Men's Clubs multiply, the establishment of penny banks, and other methods of saving which are their invariable adjuncts, will probably produce a still more remarkable increase in English savings.

But if the Post Office Savings Bank has done and is doing so much to educate the people in those habits of saving and thrift which form the elementary school for the accumulation of capital in the hands of the working-classes, Building Societies have taken us a step further, and taught the working-man not only the value of saving, but the meaning of investment, with the potent inducement to save which it presents. Hitherto they have been the greatest and most successful agent in creating 'peasant proprietors' of capital, with all that would spring from their wide extension,—the hereditary thrift and sobriety, the conservative instincts of order, the better understanding of economic laws, the independence and power of holding their own without having recourse to the ruinous expedients of strikes and unions, necessary adjuncts of 'the freebooters of labour,' and the increased sense of family affection and duty which would come with the sense of some provision having been made for wife and family on the father's death, instead of his savings dying with him except a small sum for funeral expenses, as in the case of a benefit club, leaving his family to the tender mercies of the Poor Law.

But might not the movement be immensely helped on if the importance of it, economic and moral, were duly recognized?

Mr. Seebohm, who as a banker opposes the extension of the limits imposed on the deposits at Post Office Savings Banks, contending that 'they are only intended to bring down the system of banking within reach of the working-class, not to provide them with a mode of permanent investment on a false economical principle, and therefore at a lower rate of interest than an investment on Government security ought in the open market to receive,' contends at the same time that Government can aid the people in the permanent *investment* of their savings, by placing its own public funds fairly within their reach, through the same agency of the Post

Office, which it has employed with such effect. 'It can do this,' he says, 'by acting simply as broker for the working-classes without incurring one-tenth part of the risk which is involved in acting as their bankers.' To quote his own words: 'The deposit of money by the working-classes to be returned in *money* to them on demand involves that the State should keep large floating balances uninvested to meet current demands. Recent experience has shown how apt such balances are to lie too long uninvested, and in the meantime to be temporarily, with the best intentions, misapplied. There would be no such danger in connexion with Consols. The price of £1 of Consols would be telegraphed from day to day to the various post-offices and posted up in their windows. "*The price of £1 of Consols to-day is* 18s. 6d." By each night's post the purchases and sales all over England would be advised to the head office in London. The *difference* between the total purchased and the total sold would be the amount which had to be sold or purchased by the Postmaster-General on the next day on the Post Office

THE SAVINGS QUESTION.

account. The purchases and sales of the working-classes would be matters of account in the books of the Post Office Consols department, and the whole amount under investment through the Post Office would stand in the name of the Postmaster-General in the books of the Bank of England. In the same way the dividends on the total sum would be handed over to the Postmaster-General, and distributed by him to the several holders. The Act of Parliament conferring on the Postmaster-General the necessary powers to carry out the object would, of course, have to fix the limits within which transactions were to be restricted.*

'As matters stand now Consols are not within reach of the working-classes. Dealings in Consols, through brokers, by powers of attorney and transfers with the addition of stamps and fees, are so surrounded with practical difficulties—so tied up with red tape—that they are practically

---

* A brokerage of one penny in the pound would probably pay expenses, and be a self-acting check upon the undue use of the Post Office for too large sums. The ordinary brokerage on £100 is only 2s. 6d.

out of the reach of the working classes for small amounts even in London. In very few country places are there any brokers at all, and unless a working man has access to a banker, he can hardly make a small investment in Consols. Whereas if Consols were placed within easy reach of the Post Office of every little town, the working-classes would invest their money in Consols, and get $3\frac{1}{4}$ per cent. with Government security as easily as they now get $2\frac{1}{2}$ in the Post Office Savings Bank.'

But is there not here a field for private co-operation, as well as Government aid? Taking the rate of interest given at the Post Office, do we realize how hard it would be for us to save with only $2\frac{1}{2}$ per cent. as an inducement? There are plenty of business men who have no wish to live selfish lives, with that egoism *à deux, à trois, à quatre* which our family life so plentifully supplies us with; they would gladly go beyond this narrow circle, and give some brotherly help to the working-men, on whose service all the material wants of their own life rest for their fulfilment, if they knew how. District-visiting,

THE SAVINGS QUESTION. 157

Sunday-school teaching, lecturing, teetotalism,—these are not in their line. In what better way could they help the working-classes than in aiding the accumulation of capital in their hands?

'It is not perhaps realized by persons who wish to help the working-classes in their savings,' writes Mr. Frederic Seebohm, in the article from which I have already quoted, 'how easily by means of co-operation any sound investment may be placed within their reach. A few well-to-do persons might place, say £1,000 of the debenture stock or preference shares of a first-class railway in their joint names as trustees of a co-operative investment society, and offer to sell it to small investors at the market price of the day. In the ledger of the society they would at first be entered as owners of the whole amount. As fast as investors came in they would buy from the trustees at the market price of the day small portions of the stock, until by degrees the whole £1,000 was purchased and transferred into the purchaser's names in the ledger. In the meantime the dividends would be divided among the owners, according to the amounts of stock standing in their names. With the exception of the small inconvenience of receiving the purchase-money in instalments, the whole transaction would be one of perfect safety to the original owners of the £1,000 stock, and at any time they could wind up, if needful, and get rid of further responsibility by having the amounts all transferred into the names of the purchasers in the books of the railway company, retaining the small remainder, if any, for themselves. There would be none of the risk attending a bank. The investors would have invested in railway stock paying 4 per cent. or 4½ per cent., instead of depositing their money at a savings bank at 2½ per cent. or 3 per cent. In larger places, where there might be more intelligence and business knowledge, any hundred working-men, by throwing their savings together, might soon on the same principle (without the aid of others) make co-operative investments in any security they like, and in a few years' time, when the amount of their individual investments reaches a sufficient sum, have their shares transferred into their own names.'

THE SAVINGS QUESTION. 159

The latter suggestion has been already carried out in some of our large manufacturing towns among our more intelligent artizans. But when the intelligence is wanting, I know of no more effective way of giving brotherly help than in developing a principle of thrift which, unlike benefit-club saving, does not die with the man, but, strengthened by all that is unselfish in family feeling, transmits an hereditary nest-egg to the next generation.

But surely one of the best and readiest methods of educating our people in thrift would be the establishment of a co-operative store, not upon the degenerate but familiar methods of London co-operation, but on the Rochdale plan. London co-operation only aims at saving somewhat the pockets of its customers, without affording them the inducement to acquire the habit of saving and the facility of so doing. These societies, organized chiefly to supply goods at a cheap rate, and make a large profit for the shareholders, are not co-operative in the complete sense of that term, since the managers have an interest distinct from the shareholders, and the shareholders an interest distinct from the purchasers. In Mr. George J. Holyoake's words, 'The common principle of managers, shareholders, and purchasers is that of all competitive commerce,—"each for himself and the devil take the hindermost;" and such is the activity of the devil in business that he commonly does it. Co-operation on the Rochdale method, on the other hand, is a concerted arrangement for keeping the devil out of the affair. A scheme of equity has no foremost and no hindermost for the devil to take.'* This scheme, as devised by the 'Equitable Pioneers' of Rochdale, consists in the profits made by sales, instead of being absorbed by the few who are shareholders, being divided among all the members who make purchases at the stores, in proportion to the amount they spend there; the share of the profits coming due to them remaining in the hands of the Directors until it amounts to £5. Of this amount they are registered as shareholders, and receive five per cent. interest. The store thus saves their shares for them, and they

* The 'History of Co-operation in England,' by George J. Holyoake, vol. ii., p. 136.

THE SAVINGS QUESTION. 161

become shareholders without it costing them anything. If the concern fails, they lose nothing; but if the store flourishes, and they stick like sensible men to it, they may save in the same way other five pounds which they are allowed to draw out if they please.

By this scheme the store ultimately obtains £100 of capital from every twenty members. The original capital with which to obtain the first stock was obtained, in the case of the Rochdale Pioneers, now possessing a capital of upwards of £254,000, by weekly subscriptions of twopence! For every pound so subscribed interest at the rate of 5 per cent. was promised, if the day of profits ever came. Interest was somewhat arbitrarily fixed at this rate, in order that there might be the more profit to divide among customers, as a means of attracting more members, and alluring purchasers to the store by the prospect of a quarterly dividend of profits upon their outlay. Of course those who had the largest families had the largest dealings, and the pleasing and profitable illusion was produced, that the more they ate, the more they saved.

'In commencing such a store,' says Mr. Holyoake, himself one of the bravest and most self-denying pioneers of Co-operation, and the most thorough master of its principles, 'the first thing to do is for two or three persons to call a meeting of those likely to care for the object in view and able to advance it. The callers of the meeting should be men who have clear notions of what they want to do, and how it is to be done, and why it should be attempted. Capital for the store is usually provided by each person putting down his or her name for twopence, threepence, or sixpence a week, or more, as each may be able, towards the payment of five shares of £1 each. If the store be a small one, a hundred members subscribing a one-pound share each may enable a beginning to be made. In a sound store, each member is called upon to hold five one-pound shares. It is safest for the members to subscribe their own capital. Borrowed money is a dangerous thing to deal with. Interest has to be paid often before any profits are made. Sometimes the lenders become alarmed, and call it in suddenly, which commonly breaks up the store; or the directors have to become guarantees for its repayment, and then the sole control of the store necessarily falls into their hands.... By commencing upon the system of the intending co-operators subscribing their own capital, a larger number of members is obtained, and all have an equal and personal interest in the store, and give it their custom that their money may not be lost. This plan of dividing profits on purchases secures not only a common interest, but a large and permanent custom.'*

A secretary and treasurer should be of course appointed; but perhaps the most important officers at this early stage of proceedings are two or three energetic, good-tempered collectors, who will go round and personally collect the subscriptions which are not brought to the appointed place on the appointed day. 'There is a deal of human nature in man,' as Sam Slick says, and human nature will always be slack in its stipulated payments, unless screwed up to the mark by those who have the cause sufficiently at heart to bestow much self-sacrificing labour upon it.

* The 'History of Co-operation in England,' by George J. Holyoake, vol. ii., p. 101.

If, when started, the store goes into the grocery business, or the meat trade, or tailoring, or shoemaking, or drapery, it is apparently not so hopeless as at first sight it would seem, to find a disinterested friendly grocer, or butcher, or tailor, or cordwainer, or draper, to put the co-operators into the right way of laying in and selling and preserving stock. 'Such friendly persons,' Mr. Holyoake assures us, 'are always to be found if looked for.' At first, it seems, wholesale dealers were suspicious of co-operators, and refused to deal with them. But now they are honoured customers at such firms as Messrs. J. McKenzie of Glasgow, wholesale tea-merchants; Messrs. Constable & Henderson of London, wholesale sugar-dealers; Messrs. Ward & Co. of Leeds, provision merchants. There is also a branch of the North of England's Wholesale open at 118, Minories, London, which enables a young society to offer at once to its customers goods of first-rate quality; in fact, 'to obtain West End provisions at East End prices.'

Mr. Holyoake has also some wise remarks on the necessity of treating the servants, when once appointed, with confidence and respect, never distrusting them on mere rumour or hearsay or suspicion, or on anything short of actual evidence of dishonesty. As John Stuart Mill said to the London Co-operators, 'Next to the misfortune to a society of having bad servants, is to have good servants and not know it;' and the proverbial distrust and jealousy of one another among working men forms a very serious difficulty in the successful working of a co-operative store, and many a good manager has been led by it to throw up his work in despair and disgust.

In a properly constituted store, the funds are portioned out quarterly in seven ways: (1) expenses of management; (2) interest due on all loans, if any; (3) an amount equivalent to ten per cent. of the value of the fixed stock, set apart to cover its annual reduction in worth owing to wear and tear; (4) dividends on subscribed capital of the members; (5) such sum as may be required for extension of business; (6) two and a half per cent. of the remaining profit, after all the above items are provided for, to be applied to educational purposes; (7) the residue, and that only, is then divided among all the persons employed and members of the store, in proportion to the amount of their wages or of their respective purchases during the quarter, varying from 1s. 6d. to 2s. 6d. in the pound.*

On these methods, a Co-operative store, with its ready money payments, its capitalizing of profits, and its two and a half per cent. on profits laid by for educational purposes, may be made a potent educator of the people in the all-important lessons of integrity, thrift, and self-improvement.

Into the far deeper questions of the true relations of labour and capital, whether industry is as yet organized on its right basis; whether the rise and spread of socialism does not point to left-out elements which must be brought into our social organization before our industrial problems can be solved; whether the working classes have at all their due share in the wealth of the country, I do not intend to enter, as it forms too wide a question to discuss exhaustively in these brief notes of work. But surely these questions in their

* The 'History of Co-operation in England,' by George J. Holyoake, pp. 104-5.

moral aspect are those in which the Christian Church should take a profound interest, and make herself a living voice. Whether the present principle of unlimited competition, which 'writ large' is, 'every man for himself, and the devil take the hindermost,' on which trade is based, with the inevitable slow deterioration of the quality of the work turned out, and the necessary 'scamping' it leads to, is the 'good tree' which is likely to bear good fruit; whether the conflict between capital and labour, and the selfish antagonism it leads to between identical interests, and the ruinous industrial waste of strikes, and bitter class feeling it results in, is in accordance with the great social principle of Christianity, that we are one body, and only through the co-operation of the members for the good of the organic whole can we escape from the social disorders and convulsions that must result from any schism in the body; whether the principle on which retail trade is at present based, of making the honest man pay for the knave, paying for the bad debts caused by the one with the ready money supplied by the other, is likely to educate the people in integrity and uprightness, and the habit of paying their way instead of going on trust; surely these are all vital questions relating to the kingdom of God upon earth, and which should not be left to Positivists and Secularists to take the lead in. May it not be that modern Christianity is so full of other-worldliness, has so little living grip of the rude forces that are at work in this world, so little will or knowledge to direct and control, and mould them into the living forces that make for a kingdom of God on earth,—may it not be in part owing to this, that men now-a-days go other-where than to church, to find help and guidance in the real difficulties of life?

CHAPTER VIII.

OVERCROWDING.

ON the inevitable moral evils of overcrowding and their cure, I need not dwell at such length as I have done on the drinking and the savings questions, as the Acts for the Improvement of Artizans' Dwellings have at last placed the power of dealing with it in the hands of municipal authorities. But as these Acts must be very slow in coming into operation, cannot we do something to remedy, or at least to keep in check, present evils? I ask, how is it possible for a young girl to grow up in modesty and decency, when she has been in the habit of sleeping in the same room with her father, or, worse still, her grown-up brother? Must not the outworks of a girl's chastity be fatally broken down by such practices? and have we not here the fertile germs of that immorality which is so apt to gravitate in its turn into the still graver evils, moral and sanatory, of prostitution How is it, I ask, that the most devoted Sunday-school teachers, who carefully visit their children never think of finding out whether the conditions of their homes are such as to make it possible for them to practise the Christian modesty and purity they inculcate? How is it that at mothers' meetings, professedly intended to help women to a higher standard and a better practice in their maternal duties, this care for their girls' modesty is never mentioned? Too much stress cannot be laid with mothers on two things,—decency in their girls' sleeping arrangements, and not allowing them to play with loose boys in the street. When through extreme poverty, or overcrowding, there is inevitable paucity of room, often an earnest talk with the mother on the subject, and a little friendly contrivance, the gift of a curtain or a screen from the district visitor, or the lady who holds the mothers' meeting, would obviate the worst consequences. One of our most noted temperance speakers stated to a friend of mine that he was one of eight

OVERCROWDING.

children, the mother a widow in great poverty, and only able to afford one bedroom. 'It is mere nonsense,' he said, 'to talk of indecency and immodesty being necessitated by want of room. My mother hung up a curtain right across the room, and the boys slept on one side, and she and the girls on the other; and I'll venture to say we were brought up in as much modesty and decency as richer folk with a bedroom apart for each. The poor, in the terrible pressure of existence, necessarily get careless on these points; and for what else was the higher moral training which circumstances have made possible to us, given us but to help them up to our standard, as they in their turn help us in patience and faith? Something, too, might be done by reporting any case of overcrowding, and by bringing moral pressure to bear on the landlord, through the clergyman or some other influential person. Any flagrant case can be brought under the power of the law to deal with it.

Nothing, I think, forms a much sadder spectacle, nothing more conclusively proves how little thought and care we bestow on one another, than the way in which railway companies and other agencies have been allowed to sweep away the dwellings of the poor without an attempt to furnish them with any substitute, though with the knowledge that their work would involve their living in or about the same place, with only half the accommodation, and that overcrowding and bad air must bring immorality and drinking in its train. When shall we learn in our churches and chapels that we are no more at liberty to preach the laws of moral health while all its conditions are being violated, than we are to preach the laws of physical health whilst we stop up our drains and empty our refuse into the streets? How can our moral life be anything but the mass of disorder that it is when we do not so much as attempt to train the moral emotions to a response to the most ordinary facts, when facts that simply make moral evil inevitable to the mass of men and women take place, and we do not so much as note their existence? I ask, could we solve a single scientific problem on the methods which we apply to our far more important and complex moral problems? If Dr. Tyndall had contented himself with simply saying that there *ought* to be no life in his solutions at the end of a certain period, without paying the least heed to the conditions to which they were exposed in the interim, where would be the solution of the problem of biogenesis? And when I read that he performed exactly 960 experiments in sterilising his bottles of dirty water, I exclaim, where are the 960 careful observations of all the conditions necessary for sterilising one of our moral cesspools? Where is the careful training of our moral feelings to respond to the facts that have a claim on them, as Dr. Tyndall has carefully trained his intellect to respond to the facts that appeal to it, to respond with a nicety of observation which would be an impossibility to a less cultivated mind? Can there be anything but moral confusion and disaster in such methods and such neglect in training the faculties which have been given us to guide us in conduct, a neglect which we should not think of indulging in with the faculties that are given to us to guide us in thought?

CHAPTER IX.

CONCLUSION.

MANY of us are familiar with that magnificent opening chapter of De Tocqueville's 'Democracy,' in which he traces the gradual but irresistible progress of democracy throughout modern European history. He points out how the most contradictory events, the most opposed discoveries, have alike ministered to the growth of the power of the people. The crusades, which decimated and impoverished the great feudatory families; the invention of gunpowder, that makes the common soldier a more destructive power than the Homeric chief; the invention of the printing press, which placed knowledge within reach of the humblest; in England the Wars of the Roses, which consumed the nobility; in France the policy of the kings, which in alliance with the people, humbled and subjected the nobles; the Reformation, with its vindication of the priesthood and personal responsibility of every man;—all alike ministered to the silent rise of democracy, the steady accumulation of power in the hands of the people; a process which is still silently and irresistibly going on. Whether we look on democracy as an evil or a good, whether we like it or not, the power of the people is the great inevitable fact of the future, and whether it is a Christianized fact, a power that owns that obedience to moral law which is the bond of rule, on this, in De Tocqueville's estimation, depends the future welfare of our race.

If, on the other hand, we look at Christianity with unprejudiced eyes, we are struck by the same fact, of which all European history is the evolution, hidden in the germ, and stored up, as it were, for some future use, like—

> 'the soul of the wide world
> Dreaming of things to come.'

It is very difficult for us to get rid of all adventitious associations, the traditions and ecclesiasticism of the ages, and get a glimpse of Christianity as it came fresh from the Mind and Hand of Christ, and realize its intensely democratic character. To many of us it seems irreverent even to say that He, whom we call Master and Lord, was born in an outhouse, and had only sweet-smelling hay for his first infant bed, and that for thirty of the three or four and thirty years of His life, He was only known as a thoughtful, high-minded working-man; the hands that raised the dead, and were laid in healing on the sick, being labour-hardened palms, brown with years of toil. It is difficult for us so to translate ancient forms into modern terms as to have any idea of the intensely democratic and levelling character of our Lord's teaching; how He did not hesitate to read an ecclesiastical casuist a lesson in a story in which a parson and a deacon are represented as only taking care of their own skins, but a poor infidel as risking his life and spending his money to save another, and bade the Church lawyer take the infidel for his example; how He informed an eminent member of the religious world that the poor prostitute, whose very touch he had thought defilement, had gained, through her depth of sin and anguish, a depth of love that placed her far above his self-righteous respectability; and how, on another occasion, He taught that a moral outcast of society was nearer to God than an eminently religious man noted for his attention to all his religious duties; how He once addressed the religious world as, 'Ye generation of vipers, how shall ye escape the damnation of hell?' but for the tempted, and sinful, and heavy laden people, the poor lost girls, the social outcasts, whom we respectable classes are apt to call degraded wretches, He had but the cry of yearning love, 'Come unto me, ye weary and heavy laden, and I will give you rest.' Nor is it altogether possible for us, with the glow of sacred association and passion of adoration that gathers round the Christian sacraments, to realize their true character, that dismissing all the burdensome rites and ceremonies which have ever pressed so heavily on the people, the Founder of Christianity took the two commonest actions of life, washing and eating, and made them the symbols of the awful and divine, of the very indwelling Presence of

God Himself; thereby embodying the teaching of all modern science as to the mystery, the wonder, and glory of even the natural elements of our life, of the matter which in our ignorance we used to call 'dead,' and 'brute,' and 'gross,' and making the whole of man's life sacramental, the visible sign of an inward and divine meaning. Could we better realize the democratic character of Christianity, its absolute and unique assertion of the dignity, the spiritual priesthood of man as man, apart from all social and ecclesiastical distinctions, its ecclesiastically levelling character, we should better understand how it was that the whole religious world ranged itself against Jesus Christ; that the Primate of Judea condemned Him for blasphemy, and the State, while feebly endeavouring to protect Him, at length surrendered Him to an illegal condemnation. If we do not go so far as M. Renan and say that Christianity was the inauguration of the principles of the first French Revolution, since in its reverence for law, its recognition of the great historical sources of authority even when represented by bad men, and its constant teaching that the kingdom of God is within, and cannot be secured by mere external means, but only by moral methods, it is widely opposed to the violence and externalism which has too often characterised the action of the people, yet at least we must allow that in its very nature it was the consecration of the fact of democracy, the inauguration of the fundamental principle of representative government, as opposed to the Divine right of kings and the inherent rights of aristocracies: 'He that would be chief among you, let him be the servant of all.'

If then we find Christianity and the people are in a measure separated, if an 'hospital Saturday' for the working-man has been instituted on the plea that so many of them attend neither Christian church nor chapel, if so few of them meet us at the family table of all God's children, must there not be some fault somewhere? If the intensely democratic character of Christianity is such as I have pointed out; if it was the very nature of Christ's religion that the common people heard Him gladly, and to the poor the gospel is preached; if some, like myself, have seen for themselves that it has lost none of its ancient power over the people, it suggests the grave question whether there is not something inherently lacking in our middle-class Christianity which fails to attract the working-man.

I do not think anyone much given to reflect and observe can have worked extensively among working-men without being struck by a certain difference of type which Christianity in them presents to the prevailing type of Christianity among the middle classes. Roughly delineated, the great central fact of the Christianity of the educated middle classes is personal salvation. Christianity assumes more or less the form of a Life Insurance Office, at which in return for a certain amount of faith and goodness you insure yourself against the risk of perdition hereafter. Its two factors are God and the soul; the third and equally necessary factor in primitive Christianity, the world, humanity, is almost entirely omitted, or comes in as a sort of loose after-thought, as something whose claims ought to be recognised out of gratitude for one's own personal salvation. Fortunately this feeling is so strong as often to secure the utmost devotion, at least from individuals. But it does not alter the fact that our ordinary Christianity is characterized by intense individualism, the emphatically social and corporate character of early Christianity, 'the kingdom of God,' as it was called, shrinking to the narrow limits of the individual soul, or of some particular ecclesiastical organization. Its strength lies in beauty of individual character, in what in modern times would be called moral and spiritual culture, in ancient phraseology 'edification;' its weakness, in a certain unconscious selfishness it engenders, the not very lofty ideal of getting on in this world and the next, and doing the best for yourself in both; and its inherent inability to work out any salvation for the world. The rise of Positivism, or the service of humanity, on ground which was once covered by the full tides of Christian love, but which has long been left bare and unoccupied, I think points to the truth in its broad outlines of what I say.

On the other hand, the great central fact of the Christianity of working-men is, what after all must ever be the central fact of Christianity whatever else we may make of it, a life poured out for the good of others, and personal salvation as a means to that. The conditions of their lives, the constant service in which they live, their individual weakness, and the necessity of combining into some sort of organization or body to be a power, makes them unconsciously realize Christianity under this form even in the teeth of the teaching they often receive. All the influences of their lives are opposed to individualism; their very selfishness is of a corporate character, which requires the good of the individual to be subordinated to the good of his class, and is only distinctly selfish in its action towards other classes. When once a working-man embraces Christianity, remaining as he often does very defective in moral and spiritual culture, I have often been amazed at the unconscious devotion and self-sacrifice with which he pours himself out for the public good. No fatigue after his long day's work, no excuse of late dinners or interrupted home evenings, interferes with his undertaking night after night some work to benefit his fellow-men. I remember being somewhat perplexed at recognising in the midst of much crude theology the same type of Christianity in the American evangelist, Moody, the same living grasp of that third factor 'the world,' the duty we owe those outside our own immediate circle, the same assertion that the motto of every living Christian is that of the Heir-apparent, 'I serve;' that holiness, as the word denotes, is but spiritual health, and, like health, is an end that is only a larger means, an end to be attained in order to be used. My perplexity to know how he came by this type of Christianity was cut short on opening his biography, and finding that he was by birth and bringing up a working-man pure and simple.

Now if what I have said is true, not with regard to exceptional individuals, but to classes, it is no wonder that middle-class Christianity should have so little attraction for working-men. It is not *their* Christianity. It does not possess the features to which they respond. They miss any living voice and guidance in the difficulties which the world presents to them, any keen sense even of the problems which they are often blunderingly endeavouring to solve, and which press so heavily upon them,—problems which, from their individual importance being weaker than ours, always take more or less a social form. They miss any intelligent sympathy, any real living help towards the solution of their problems, and towards establishing a kingdom of righteousness on the earth,—they miss sacrifice taken as the one foundation, the life poured out for the good of the world.

But is it not possible for these two types of Christianity, each imperfect without the other, to coalesce, for the moral and spiritual culture of the one to take up into itself the service, the self-devotion, and self-spending of the other, and so from the broken light of true Christianity to orb into the perfect 'bright and morning' star, which would herald a new dawn, not only for the working-classes, but for all classes alike? Cannot each of us do much to bring in a fuller, truer Christianity, which will draw all men unto it, a Christianity that possesses the three essential factors, God, the individual soul, and the world?

Those of us who have the care and training of boys, cannot we bring them up from the

CONCLUSION.

earliest years, not with the one idea of getting on in life, and making money, taking care to save their own souls if they can in the process; but with the sense that they were sent into the world for a purpose, for a work, not merely 'to be born red and die grey,' but to leave the world a little the better for a noble life and a work well done? Cannot we bring them up to realize that all good and conscientious work is Church work, work done for the kingdom of God,—that the lawyer serves the Just One, the physician fulfils His command, 'Heal the sick,' the scientific man reveals Him as the faithful and true, in whom is no shadow of variableness or turning? Surely we need not fall into that melancholy confusion, that because we like our work, or make a good thing out of it, therefore we do it for ourselves, and not for the world. This seems to me to be the very dregs of asceticism, with all that is high and noble in it left out. Man is so made for service that he *must* find pleasure in his work. The pleasure and profit are thrown in as the tradesman throws in the paper and the twine that enfold some precious thing. But to say that the paper and twine is all we care about is surely false. Considering the strength of the social instincts in man, considering the absolute self-devotion to the most unworthy ends which has been successfully inculcated, surely I am not visionary in believing that the noblest of all ends—the service of humanity—might be so inculcated from earliest boyhood, so bound up with the thought of God in the soul, so fortified by all the internal and external sanctions that life affords, that it might become the ruling passion, absorbing into itself all lower passions, and giving those wider horizons to our most circumscribed work which impart to all life something of the exhilaration of a mountain climb. It is that our Christianity is so feeble, so negative, so self-circumscribed, so peeping and peering, and full of fears for itself, so wanting in bold heroic outlines and strong passions, that it has so little power over young men either in our own class or among working-men.

And our girls, with their fair culture, their pretty homes, their graceful accomplishments with their amusements, and their pleasant excursions abroad, or by the seaside, and all the charm of social intercourse; with all the good influences, and tender care, and sheltered purity which have surrounded them; all the delights of happy girlhood which 'fetch the day about from sun to sun, and rock the year as in a delightsome dream,'—cannot we wake up in their hearts the question, 'What right have I to all this? what right, when other girls as young and fair, and with the same thought in their hearts, that they can be young only once, have to stand week in week out at the washtub, or toil in crowded factories or stifling work-rooms?' Cannot we teach them what a young, generous heart is so quick to learn, that they hold all their advantages as a trust for those who have none, and that their lot is so bright to enable them to let a little of its pleasant sunshine flow over into some dark young heart, whose pleasures, the street and the dancing saloon, are even sadder than its griefs; or even into those monotonous lives of toil so many good girls are leading around them?

That we so utterly fail to teach this to so many of our girls, may it not be that we have forgotten it in some measure ourselves—forgotten the fact which one of our poets has so exquisitely expressed for us, speaking of the people—

> 'Our lives are beautiful thro' drudgeries
> Of theirs which left them rest and space to grow
> Thro' generations to the perfect curve ;
> Our hair has got the gold because the dust
> Of the world's highways never soiled the feet
> Of our forefathers ; and the blue-veined hands
> Were moulded to their tenderness of touch
> By centuries of service rude and hard.'

Too often in the selfish isolation of our well-to-do homes and family life, we do not recognize that the blue-veined hands were thus moulded ' by centuries of service rude and hard ' that they might be the whiter and the tenderer to lift the poor lost girl out of the mire of her sins, and be laid in healing touches on all human sorrow; that if through the drudgeries of the people we have had rest and space to grow to our full moral and intellectual stature, it must be that we might be the stronger to help up the debased and the ignorant ; that if on us is the fine gold of refinement and culture, through the leisure purchased for us by their toil, it must be that we should have more to give, more wherewith to enrich their lives and ours, than if we all were dirty, and ignorant, and ugly, in back streets together: But alas! we lose sight of the relation of our lives to other lives; we leave out the facts which have determined our condition in the present, and should shape them to noble uses in the future; we spend our trust money, regarding only the coin, and disregarding the trust. We first surround ourselves with every comfort and refinement, and then stretch out our hands to help others with what we may chance to have left, placing as an ornament at the top what should be as a base at the foundation; and then we wonder that our good life is such a failure, that our Christianity has so little power to draw all men to it.

I believe myself that an immense movement is already setting in towards a more organic Christianity, a Christianity that will recognise generally what, thank God, many individuals have already recognised, that we are members of one organic whole, and that the limb can only attain to its true health and joyous activity by losing itself in serving the whole, in other words by bringing in that very factor, the world, humanity, which we have left out, a Christianity which would build up a moral order on somewhat the same methods as science has built up an intellectual order in our life, by training the moral emotions to respond to fact, as men have already trained the intellectual faculties. It will not be left to Positivism to teach that we are each one born under a load of obligations of every kind, obligations to our predecessors, to our successors, to our contemporaries; that after our birth these obligations increase and accumulate, since it is some time before we can render any service, but have to be supported at the expense of others. Even when we are old enough to take our place in the world, whatever our work and whatever our success in that work, such success depends in the main on the co-operation of others, without which we should be left naked and hungry, and homeless and helpless; and that to live for others, therefore, is for all of us a constant duty, the rigorous logical consequence of an indisputable fact, the fact, viz., that we live by others. I believe we shall not leave it to Positivism to recognize that the facts of our life deprive us of all individual rights but one, the right to do our duty, the right that enables us to do our appointed service in the world. I believe that the time is coming when 'duty,' not selfish 'rights,' will become the watchword of humanity; and when a fuller Christianity will be able so to mould public opinion that the man who lives simply for his own pleasure and amusement, in enjoyment of the rights of property, will be branded as a man who has lived a pauper at the public expense, and died without an attempt to pay his debts; a time when it will be as much ground into a man by education and religious influences that he has got to fulfil his obligations to humanity, to others, as it now is that he has got to fulfil his obligations to himself and to his own soul. In one word, I believe a Christianity is coming which will teach us not only our relations to God, but our relations to His world,— not only our relations through Christ to God, but also our relations through Christ to humanity, of whom He is equally the representative; a Christianity which will base itself less upon theological dogma and more upon the facts of life.

I can only earnestly beseech parents not to stand in the way of this higher life for their children, a joy which the world can neither give nor take away. I would humbly and earnestly remind them 'whose they are and whom they serve,' even One who spared not His own Son, but freely gave Him up for us all; and beseech them not to refuse to give up their children in return to God. So far from really giving them up, parents too often will not let their children give up a single *convenance* of the world, or put them to the least inconvenience or privation for the sake of Him who gave up His well-beloved Son to shame and stripes and nakedness and death for them. Many a girl would have thankfully lived a less frivolous, objectless life, but her parents objected to her walking alone to the place where her help is wanted, not for fear of any real harm befalling her, as far more unprotected working-class girls go safely to and fro to their work, but simply from fear of the world and what will be said. Or it is not convenient to give up a room in the house where she might invite some of the poor tempted girls in the neighbourhood, and be an untold blessing to them as a friend and companion ; it would put the family out, and therefore it is out of the question. Or the girls of the house are not to take any evening work, because they are wanted at home to play and sing and look pretty, or it would interfere with the late dinner. Or perhaps, having been the companion of her brothers, a girl feels she knows more about boys, and while she does not care about girls, she would thankfully undertake a class of rough lads, to whom she, with her refinement, her purity, her devotion, would be literally an angel from heaven. But service being scarcely thought of, and the world being with us early and late, and it being a received though unexpressed maxim that no risk must be run for the kingdom of God, such a thing cannot be heard of for a moment. Is there not at least some truth in James Hinton's sarcastic observation that 'the devil always comes to an Englishman in the shape of his wife and family'? From the very strength of our family instincts, our family selfishness is the hardest thing we have to overcome. The hardest thing is not to give up ourselves, but to give up our dear ones to God, to let them run counter to the world, and be talked about, and encounter evil and impurity with only the God we profess to believe in to keep them safe while they are about their Father's business.

Yet what is the result of our thinking that we can keep them safer in our homes than God can in His service? Some of us who are set apart by some unconscious influence to be the confessors of our kind know all that goes on in many of our outwardly pure and cultured homes,—the envy, the jealousies, the spite, the hidden impurity, which like a moral smallpox is ravaging many a fair young soul, simply from want of any higher passion to cast out and consume the lower. Were it not better to use the evils without to destroy the evils within?—not to insist on their living in a sheltered dreamland, nor try to

> ' build up about their soothèd sense a world
> That is not God's, and wall them up in dreams,
> So their young hearts may cease to beat with His,
> The great world-heart, whose blood for ever shed
> Is human life, whose ache is man's dumb pain;'

but believing that God's world must be better than our dreamland, and will work out in them a better goodness than we can, with bold faith to send them out to do battle in it for the kingdom of God, and to help, to serve, and to save, suffering its mighty forces to mould them to heroic shape, and give them both joys and sorrows deeper and more blessed than any we can give.

May I not plead the example of my own father, who, occupying a prominent position in the University, and in the world of science, which necessarily made those who belonged to him more or less conspicuous, yet in a place where it was confessedly more objectionable for a girl to be talked about than in any other, gave up his only unmarried daughter to the service of the rough men about us, suffered me to go alone into public-houses, and to beat about the streets at night, voluntarily foregoing the companionship he loved, and only holding himself in readiness to counsel and uphold me in every difficulty and opposition I encountered? It was a great sacrifice made for God, far greater than sacrificing himself. But it brought life from the dead to many of those rough men, and Christian influences to many a little child; it brought an untold blessing to my own soul; and it has ever made that one word 'Father' that in which I can best utter my highest love and adoration. May I not plead with parents to go and do likewise?

And to any young folk who may read these brief notes and suggestions on work, I would say, try this joyous life of service. Do not rush into any great undertaking at first. I did not begin with six hundred working-men, but with six girls of my own age. But let there be no bounds to your devotion and earnestness in what you do undertake, remembering that 'I can't' is a lie on the lips that repeat 'I believe in the Holy Ghost.' Pray, and all things in the line of God's will shall be possible to you. And don't mind being in a fright; I don't think any one can have endured greater agonies of terror than I have; and a good thing too, as it casts one more entirely on God's strength. To girls I would say, if you are perplexed how to begin, begin as I did, with asking six or seven respectable girls, daughters of washerwomen, or young dressmakers, to tea on Sunday, to read your Bible together; don't preach to them, but share your upward struggles with them, and get to know them and try to be their friend. You will find, through being their own age, you can help them better than we older folk. Or, if you are of a more adventurous disposition, get together some of the back-street girls, or rough lads, and see whether, by gaining their affections, you cannot get them into shape. Trust me, you will find scope enough for any amount of heroism that may be in you, in overcoming your difficulties, till at last you are able to rejoice before the Eternal with the joy of angels.

And years and years hence, when you have grown old, and sit with your faded hands folded in the twilight musing over your past life, see if the fairest, sweetest, most lasting joy is not that early labour of love that first swept you out of yourself into the very life of God, which is the redemption of the world.

BY THE SAME AUTHOR.

LIFE AND LETTERS OF JAMES HINTON.
Edited by ELLICE HOPKINS. With an Introduction by Sir WILLIAM W. GULL.

Fourth Edition. Crown 8vo, cloth, 8s. 6d.

"The life of James Hinton, the first aural surgeon of his time, presents a striking study of character, and will be instructive, in its simpler outlines, to readers who are unable to follow the deeper and somewhat mystic course of philosophical thought traced in his 'Letters.'"—*Saturday Review.*

"James Hinton's biography has fallen into good hands. . . . The book is full of interest, and by no means void of instruction. We have the clearest conviction that he was a good man,—an exceptionally, illustriously good man."—*Spectator.*

"We may add that Miss Hopkins has executed a difficult task with great tact. She shows a hearty appreciation of her subject, and her work is well done."—*Pall Mall Gazette.*

"We commend this book to all thoughtful readers."—*Guardian.*

"Miss Ellice Hopkins has done her part as editor, by a happy intermixture of biography and epistle, with admirable good sense and good taste, for which every true student of medical science and religious philosophy will be warmly grateful."—*Standard.*

KEGAN PAUL, TRENCH & CO.

ROSE TURQUAND: A NOVEL.
Third and Cheaper Edition, price 6s.

"Shows real power, and no little originality."—*Times.*
"A book to be read and re-read."—*Westminster Review.*

MACMILLAN & CO.

CHRIST THE CONSOLER:
A BOOK OF COMFORT FOR THE SICK AND SORROWFUL.

Third Edition. Foolscap, cloth, 6s.

"Its structure is a kind of dialogue between the disciple and the Consoler. The disciple states his case, and the thoughts and feelings which it occasions; the Consoler replies. The conception and execution are equally true. It is a nice and precious *vade mecum* for sufferers."—*British Quarterly.*

LONGMANS & CO.

OCCUPATION FOR THE SICK;
Or, PRACTICAL SUGGESTIONS FOR INVALIDS AND THOSE WHO HAVE THE CARE OF THEM.

Second Edition. 16mo, cloth, price 1s.

"Exquisitely and gracefully written. It answers fully, in short, to its second title, and to all this second class in particular we recommend this little book as one that will prove an unspeakable help in their difficult avocation."—*Guardian.*

WORK IN BRIGHTON:
A WOMAN'S MISSION TO WOMEN.

Eighteenth Thousand. 16mo, paper cover, price 6d. Post free.

"From my own experience in long past years I am quite sure that the way indicated in 'Work in Brighton' is the only true way; and I would entreat the women of England to read the little book, and then judge each for herself in what way she can help the cause which, for the sake of home and family, has a claim on every woman."—*Florence Nightingale.*

HATCHARDS.

BY THE SAME AUTHOR.

VILLAGE MORALITY.
A Letter to Clergymen's Wives and Christian Workers.
Price 6d. (50 *copies at half-price.*)

ON THE EARLY TRAINING OF OUR GIRLS AND BOYS.
Price 4d. (12 *copies at* 3d.)

ACTIVE SERVICE; OR, WORK AMONG OUR SOLDIERS.
Twenty-third Edition. 16mo, cloth, 1s. Post free.

NOTES ON PENITENTIARY WORK.
Crown 8vo, wrapper, price 6d.

"To all who are interested in this momentous subject we recommend this little work, which will be found to offer some very wise suggestions, the fruit of large experience, dictated by a broad love of souls."—*Literary Churchman.*

A PLEA FOR THE WIDER ACTION OF THE CHURCH OF ENGLAND
IN THE PREVENTION OF THE DEGRADATION OF WOMEN,
As submitted to the Committee of Convocation, held July 3rd, 1879.
Fourth Edition. Crown 8vo, sewed, price 3d.

PREVENTIVE WORK; OR, THE CARE OF OUR GIRLS.
Sixth Edition.
HATCHARDS.

LADIES' ASSOCIATION FOR THE CARE OF FRIENDLESS GIRLS:
Being an Account of the Work in Brighton. (Reprinted from the "Day of Rest."
Ninth Thousand. 18mo, 1d.

FRED. WILLIAMS: A TALE FOR BOYS.
Fourth Edition. 1s. 6d.
JARROLD & SON.

HOME THOUGHTS FOR MOTHERS AND MOTHERS' MEETINGS.
Fifth Edition. Price 1s. 6d.
JAMES NISBET & CO.

DOES IT ANSWER? A WORD FOR SOLDIERS.
Second Edition. Price 1d.
PARTRIDGE & CO.

www.ingramcontent.com/pod-product-compliance
Lightning Source LLC
Chambersburg PA
CBHW020913230426
43666CB00008B/1435